W9-CGP-172

365

DEVOTIONS

—— *for* ——

CATHOLICS

Creative Communications for the Parish
1564 Fencorp Drive
Fenton, MO 63026
www.creativecommunications.com

365 Devotions for Catholics: Daily Moments with God
was compiled by Terence Hegarty and Paul Pennick
for Creative Communications for the Parish,
1564 Fencorp Drive, Fenton, MO 63026. 800-325-9414.

www.livingfaith.com
www.creativecommunications.com

ISBN: 978-1-68279-130-1

Cover photo: Shutterstock.com
Cover design: Lindsey Galvin

Printed in the U.S.A.

Other books by *Living Faith* include:

Living Faith: Prayers for Catholics

Reading God's Word

Living Faith Kids: Set of Sticker Booklets

Praying the Mass

Learning about the Sacraments

Praying the Rosary

Learning All About Mary

Meet Pope Francis

Meet Mother Teresa

Learning About the Ten Commandments

Praying the Stations of the Cross

What I See in Church

Living the Beatitudes

All About Angels

What We Do in Advent

What We Do in Lent

Learning About the Works of Mercy

TABLE OF CONTENTS

INTRODUCTION

> This is the day the LORD has made;
> let us be glad and rejoice in it. Psalm 118:24

Words have power. They influence our thoughts, our emotions and
our actions. A talented novelist can make us laugh or cry. An inves-
tigative journalist reporting on injustices can make us angry. But
no words have more power than the Word of God. And no person
is more powerful than Jesus, the Word Made Flesh.

By gifting us with his word, God invites us every day to walk
with him, to seek him and to constantly better ourselves. In the
pages that follow, you will find inspiring, challenging and thought-
provoking devotions to accompany you each day of the entire year.

By reflecting on God's word, we can come to enjoy a greater
prayer life and deepen our relationship with God, creating a bond
that transcends language and logic. With *365 Devotions for Catholics*, our *Living Faith: Daily Catholic Devotions* authors are hoping
that their everyday experiences—their joys, their sorrows, their
struggles—can help readers on their own journey with God. What
you will find here are some of the very best reflections that have
appeared in the pages of *Living Faith* over the last several years.

As Catholics, we count the 40 days of Lent in anticipation of
the joy of Easter, we count the 28 days of Advent and the number

of shopping days until Christmas. Some count the days until their retirement.

But in all of that "counting down," let us take a few moments daily, through these devotions, to remember that each day is a gift. A day should not be something to simply count down or get through. It is precious—every single day that we are granted life is sacred. Every day, every hour, every minute, every second is a gift from God.

Let this book serve as a tangible reminder that what we do with our time really does matter—every day.

Enjoy the journey!

Terence Hegarty
Editor, *Living Faith: Daily Catholic Devotions*

A Prayer of St. Paul

I kneel before the Father, from whom every family in heaven and on earth is named, that he may grant you in accord with the riches of his glory to be strengthened with power through his Spirit in the inner self, and that Christ may dwell in your hearts through faith; that you, rooted and grounded in love, may have strength to comprehend with all the holy ones what is the breadth and length and height and depth, and to know the love of Christ that surpasses knowledge, so that you may be filled with all the fullness of God...to him be glory in the church and in Christ Jesus to all generations, forever and ever. Amen.

Ephesians 3:14-19, 21

'In Memory of Me'

I remember the deeds of the Lord. Psalm 77:12

If you're looking for a life-changing biblical verse to grab on to, here it is. Do this, and your life will surely be different.

To remember what God has done—his creating, his saving, his sending the Spirit—is to view our life in the context of reality. Only then can we see our way forward. If we forget what God has done, we neglect reality; inevitably, we go astray.

How do we remember? Above all, we remember in the Mass. Not simply a remembering of a past event, the Mass is the great remembering in which Christ's sacrifice again becomes present to us. We remember that God has created us, that he has sent his Son to us, that his Son has given his life for us and for all. But we each need our own ways of remembering. For the psalmist, it is a matter of meditating and pondering (Psalm 77:13).

What means will you or I use today to remember the deeds of the Lord?

Kevin Perrotta

Sharing the Wealth Today

> But God said to him, "You fool, this night your life will be demanded of you; and the things you have prepared, to whom will they belong?" Luke 12:20

Who doesn't sympathize with the man who wanted to hoard his harvest to enjoy later? We've heard time and again of the need to save for the future.

But God also calls us to live in the present. Thinking you'll volunteer every week at a homeless shelter once the kids are out of the house? Volunteer an hour or two a month now. Thinking you'll spend an hour a day in prayer once you retire? Pray ten minutes on the way to work or the grocery store today.

The plans we make for the future have a way of being turned on their heads. Let's resolve to share our gifts responsibly and as fully as possible today rather than waiting for "someday."

Lord, help me be present to your will today and every day.

Melanie Rigney

Noticing Goodness

He must increase; I must decrease. John 3:30

This line of John the Baptist about Jesus can serve as powerful spiritual direction for us in these times that are significantly challenging for many, whether with economic and employment crises or with the other strains and losses of daily living. It is easy to be overwhelmed with the difficulties, constantly working the problems, feeling the fear close in. "He must increase; I must decrease" could be a mantra, as we deliberately focus in this moment on the immediate presence of God's saving love rather than turning our attention in dread to the threat of what frightens us.

What helps me the most to do this is to try to notice any aspect of goodness right here in this moment—anything beautiful or peaceful or delicious or interesting or encouraging or kind. Noticing goodness makes my awareness of God's presence increase and my fear-gripped sense of self decrease.

Beloved God, please help me to live increasingly in trust, knowing ever more deeply that you are right here with me now and always.

Patricia Livingston

True Satisfaction

They all ate and were satisfied. Mark 6:42

We're in the week of rude awakenings. Our lives are getting back to normal after Thanksgiving, Advent, Christmas and New Year's. Many of us spent too much money trying to fill emotional and physical holes with family and friends. Now we've found the holes are still there, along with new ones in our bank accounts. No matter how noble or selfless our intentions, excess in this world doesn't satisfy long-term.

The disciples despaired at the cost of feeding the crowd, saying they'd need 200 days of wages. And yet, they learned that with Christ, five loaves and two fish were more than sufficient.

As we work on resolutions to spend, eat and drink less, may we also resolve to trust more in the Master's love, which feeds and satisfies like nothing else.

Lord, I praise your name. True satisfaction begins and ends with you.

Melanie Rigney

When Enough Is Enough

What profit is there for one to gain the whole world yet lose or forfeit himself? Luke 9:25

It's possible to accumulate so much of "the world" that you lose your own "self." We expend so much time, effort and psychic energy trying to fortify our lives with the things of this world; we would do well to be on guard that we don't gain too much of this stuff. We live in the world, of course, and everyone has a right to food, clothing, shelter, education, rest and restful recreation, personal safety and so forth. But it's possible to get to a point where these things smother our deepest and truest selves.

So be careful that you don't gain too much of a good thing. In this new year, pray for the wisdom to recognize when enough is enough. As long as there are people who don't have anywhere near enough, of course, there will always be opportunities to share because nobody deserves too much of a good thing.

Lord Jesus, help me see when enough is enough.

Mitch Finley

Being Reborn

Let your kindness comfort me,
  according to your promise to your servants. Psalm 119:76

Being born occurs throughout our lives. We emerge from darkness many times. Like that first trip through the birth canal, we never make it on our own. We come from mothers and lots of others. Self-creation is the myth; everyone needs a push and prayer to reach the light. When we cannot see the way ahead, a word may find us. Groans give way to gratitude. Compassion is real. The unfolding of a life pauses at death and then moves onward.

Being here is the gift, but it's not always apparent. We fall down. Someone must be to blame, and perhaps it is God. We can dig ourselves in deep before we remember to look up. Every pit opens to the sky.

We wanted to have it all, and we failed. But it's surprising how well what is broken catches the light. God, bring me to life in the spirit of compassion.

Jeanne Schuler

Paying Homage to God

On entering the house they saw the child with Mary his mother. They prostrated themselves and did him homage.

Matthew 2:11

A cherished Christmas tradition in our family was my father's reading aloud to us Henry Van Dyke's haunting story, *The Other Wise Man*. I have never forgotten the message of that tale of the fourth Magi, Artaban. He was to journey with the others, following the great star to pay homage to the King. On his way to meet their caravan, he stops to care for a dying stranger by the road. When he reaches the meeting place, they have left without him.

For thirty-three years he wanders, searching, feeling he has failed. In all his travels, he finds people needing rescue, healing, comfort, food, shelter. As he is dying, a tender voice assures him that whatever he did for the least of these, he did for the One he sought.

We, like Artaban, do not see the actual epiphany of the Divine. But on all the pathways of our journey, we meet and do him homage in our moments of compassion: feeding the hungry, caring for the sick, reading children stories that touch their hearts forever.

Patricia Livingston

WORDS THAT LAST

Heaven and earth will pass away, but my words will not pass away. Mark 13:31

Spoken twenty centuries ago, the words of Jesus have not passed away. They have been passed along from one generation to the next, from one country to another. His words have instructed millions in the ways of holiness, inspired the discouraged and consoled those who have faced pains and sorrows. Jesus can offer the eternal guarantee that his words will not pass away because he will not pass away. His words are the good news that neither time can diminish nor death destroy.

Some day earth and sky will disappear. The sun will make its last delivery of heat and light. The remnants of our beautiful planet will turn into stellar dust, but the words of the Lord will still exist. They promise life beyond comprehension, happiness beyond imagination and eternal security in the great beyond.

We praise you, Lord, for your words give us spirit and life.

Fr. James McKarns

Our Stream of Life-Giving Water

Blessed is the man who trusts in the Lord...
   He is like a tree planted beside the waters
      that stretches out its roots to the stream. Jeremiah 17:7-8

On our provincial house property, we have a huge oak tree estimated to be 300 years old. It towers so far above the other trees that you can't even see its top. Its trunk is so massive it takes about five adults with outstretched arms to encircle it. One secret to its longevity and size is the stream that runs nearby. This incredible tree has the good fortune of being rooted next to a generous supply of water.

What about us? Do we stay close to our "spiritual water supply," that is, Scripture, the Eucharist, prayer, family, friends, nature and our loving service of others? If so, thank God! If not, what draws us away?

God, help me to stay rooted in you.

Sr. Melannie Svoboda, S.N.D.

Settling Into the Arms of God

God is love, and whoever remains in love remains in God and God in him. 1 John 4:16

This verse is one of the best doorways for me into the mystery that is God. It helps me understand that in all my experiences of love, I have actually been shown God: in the tenderness with which my mother wiped my face when I was very sick, in the delight of a grandchild running toward me with her arms out, in the way friends and family have stood with me, heart and soul, in times of trouble and of rejoicing.

Remaining in love is remaining in God, John tells us. I recently read that the Greek word translated here as "remain in" can also be translated as "settle in for a while and relax." In these challenging times, I am grateful to be reminded to settle in for a while into all the ways that love is in my life and feel myself relax, knowing that I am settling into the arms of God.

Patricia Livingston

Sing Praise to the Lord

Sing to the LORD a new song,
    for he has done wondrous deeds. Psalm 98:1

Sometimes gratitude and earnest devotion just aren't enough to express how we feel about our relationship with God. Only singing praise seems adequate. Music is powerful. Every year when I bring carols to folks in a nursing home, I see song break through and touch hearts where words cannot.

St. Augustine is credited with saying, "A person who sings prays twice." Beautiful music itself is prayer, and when wedded to words of praise, the result is a foretaste of the new Earth to come. This can be true whether it is plainchant, choral music or a modern composition (though we all have preferences).

Except for a few holiday events, do you sing joyfully or do you just listen to the choir or mouth the words timidly at Mass? Christmas carols are behind us, but let us continue to "sing joyfully to the Lord...break into song; sing praise."

Phil Fox Rose

Take Grief to the Lord

... but a double portion to Hannah because he loved her, though the Lord had made her barren. 1 Samuel 1:5

Barrenness can be defined in many ways, not just the inability to have a child. Barrenness can mean brokenness, unfulfilled dreams, empty parts of your heart, dashed hopes, neglected passions, anything that hasn't turned out the way you'd planned. Like Hannah, we all grieve the areas of our life that aren't showing signs of growth.

The important thing about grief is to know where to take it: to God. He can handle the full weight of our grief, the total measure of our frustration and disappointment. Go ahead, vent. But in the wake of that expression of emotion, it is crucial to maintain an open, trusting heart. Barrenness is not always a permanent state for those who trust in the Lord; Hannah later had a son named Samuel.

Pour your heart out to the Lord and dedicate your future fulfillment to him. Have faith as each chapter of your story is written. Our God specializes in the impossible.

Kristin Armstrong

Loving Jesus

Everyone is looking for you. Mark 1:37

When we begin relationships, they are sometimes based on what an individual does for us. For example, we might have a connection with someone who helps us at work or assists in carpooling our children. But if the relationship stays on this level, it remains limited. Friendships deepen when we begin to appreciate individuals for themselves. When we start to value a person for who he or she simply is, the relationship moves to a deeper level.

So, too, our relationship with Jesus. In this gospel, "everyone is looking" for Jesus because he healed people. Such miracles were exciting, and a large crowd began to follow him. But eventually, Jesus asks a demanding question: "Do you love me?" The saints eventually came to love Jesus, not for what he did for them, but simply for who he is.

Today, when you have a quiet moment, "look" at the Lord in your heart and "see" his radiant beauty...and love him, just for himself.

Msgr. Stephen J. Rossetti

SOMETHING BETTER

**Does the LORD so delight in holocausts and sacrifices
as in obedience to the command of the LORD?
Obedience is better than sacrifice...** 1 Samuel 15:22

Obedience may well be better than sacrifice, but it's also a whole lot harder. To write a check, spend a few hours of service to a cause or even open my house in hospitality is a small sacrifice compared to trying to love my neighbor or pray for those who persecute me. (Okay, I'm not really persecuted, but I am mightily annoyed at times.)

When obedience is required by Church laws and regulations, it's easy to chafe under the restriction. Can't I just tithe, and then do what I want? No, says Samuel, you can't—not if you want to delight the Lord.

And not if you want any relationship that isn't merely one-sided. Obedience means yielding our will, a most prized possession, for the sake of a demand that comes from outside of us. That, in itself, can be a healthy exercise in acknowledging something greater than ourselves.

Lord, help me to live, not just hear, your word.

Mark Neilsen

In-Depth Healing

The Pharisees and their scribes complained to his disciples, saying, "Why do you eat and drink with tax collectors and sinners?" Luke 5:30

Tax collectors worked for the Romans. Mistrusted for many reasons, they inhabited the fringes of the community. When Jesus called him, Levi stood up and walked away from his tax table forever. He knew he was lost. He was ready when the invitation finally arrived. That night he threw a party for Jesus and for the other tax collectors to celebrate.

The most dangerous and common form of despair on the journey of faith, says one philosopher, is unconscious: We are carried along by events, never discovering our deepest selves. Spiritual health comes only to those who acknowledge their weakness and seek help.

The Pharisees did not seek help. Mired in self-righteousness, they did not know the freedom of those who have been found. The tax collectors' party confounded them.

God, please heal me so that I may join the party.

Jeanne Schuler

THE TRUTH HEALS

You will know the truth, and the truth will set you free.

John 8:32

We all have those moments, the kind we cannot escape. When the thing we have been praying about, the confrontation or conversation we have been hoping to avoid, is suddenly in our face. Blocking our path, it is a divinely opened door, the alignment of circumstances, the undeniable thump on the back from the Holy Spirit.

These are the moments when all our reading, all our praying, all our studies have to be "walked" out in real life. These are the moments when character is forged. And in that moment, when we are called either to speak the truth or to hear it, we are set free. No matter how uncomfortable, how awkward, how painful, how raw or how long it takes, the truth heals.

Kristin Armstrong

GOD'S POWER TO TRANSFORM

But if the wicked man turns away from all the sins he committed, if he keeps all my statutes and does what is right and just, he shall surely live, he shall not die. Ezekiel 18:21

Consistently doing what is right and just is no easy task, and we may feel overwhelmed by the difficulty at times. But we are not alone in the struggle. One of the great messages of holy Scripture is that God is always with us in our struggles. The more we open our hearts to God's power, the more successful we become in doing what is right and just.

The power of God is always within us, helping us to do those things that will bring peace both to ourselves and to others. In my difficult moments, I imagine that his power is shining within me and throughout my entire being. The more I concentrate on that image, the more it takes over and transforms my life.

Lord, may I never forget that your transforming power is always within me.

Fr. Kenneth Grabner, C.S.C.

A LESSON IN BEAUTY

Look up at the sky and count the stars, if you can.

Genesis 15:5

Growing up a city kid in St. Louis, I still vividly remember those occasional weekends spent in rural Missouri. I recall my father telling me to go outside and count the stars, and to this day I don't know if he was just trying to keep me busy or teach me a priceless lesson. Whatever the motive, the lesson stuck. I still cannot look at a bright, starry sky and not think of the endless and majestic power of creation and, more importantly, the Creator. I still cannot count the stars, and neither can I fathom such a work of beauty and immensity without attributing it to the ultimate source of life and light. Always, stars lead me to the wonders of God.

Creator God, thank you for the brilliant beacons that point me to you.

Steve Givens

ALL WE HAVE IS GIFT

Give and gifts will be given to you...shaken down, and over-flowing... Luke 6:38

It's an odd thing in our culture that the most generous among us are so often those with the least. Maybe they already know that what they have is gift. They know they're not entitled to it, so they are willing to share with those around them. Affluence seems to cloud this knowledge: The more we have, the more we seem to have a sense of entitlement. "I've worked hard to get where I am" is a sentiment we affluent tend to have, as though working hard were enough.

But each of us who has "made it" has to have had some break, some opportunity that others didn't have or couldn't take advantage of for reasons beyond themselves. No one is truly self-made. Indeed, we have already been showered with gifts "shaken down, and overflowing." I pray that all of us can someday see that everything we have is gift and give to others out of the great abundance God promises.

Aileen O'Donoghue

Tears of Remembrance

I yearn to see you again, recalling your tears... 2 Timothy 1:4

I joined a human rights delegation traveling to Haiti in 1993, a time of widespread political unrest. Our role was to listen. We were to document the struggle for peace and democracy. Although we had a thorough orientation prior to our arrival, there was nothing that could have truly prepared us for what we saw, heard and experienced.

By the third night, my heart was saturated by human suffering, and I began to weep: for those who had risked their lives simply to speak with us; for the malnourished children weak from hunger; for the profound hospitality we had received from so many who possessed so few material belongings.

I prayed that my tears would be a holy water of sorts, blessing my new neighbors and cleansing my heart and my worldview of attitudes of entitlement. And I prayed that, like St. Paul, I would forever recall those tears.

Loving God, bless those for whom and with whom I weep, and remember them in your heart.

Sr. Chris Koellhoffer, I.H.M.

TAKING NOTHING FOR GRANTED

Amen, I say to you, no prophet is accepted in his own native place. Luke 4:24

There is something in humanity that makes us take the familiar for granted—whether the familiar is a person, place or thing. We rave over the guest speaker, for example, but overlook the fine speakers in our midst. We marvel at the flowers in the botanical gardens, but miss the forsythia in our own backyard. We travel hundreds of miles to see a geological wonder, but fail to notice the geological wonders of our own area—rivers, trees, plains, rocks, hills.

We might ask ourselves: Is there a person close to home I am taking for granted? If so, how might I show my appreciation for him or her today? Are there things around me I am dismissing as ordinary when, in fact, they are quite extraordinary? Why not take a mental inventory of these things today while giving thanks to God for them?

Jesus of Nazareth, you took nothing for granted. Help me to see the people, places and things of my world today through your eyes.

Sr. Melannie Svoboda, S.N.D.

DISCERNING OUR GIFTS

There are different kinds of spiritual gifts but the same Spirit.

1 Corinthians 12:4

What Paul is talking about in this passage are particular charisms, or gifts, being discerned by the Corinthian Christians. It's natural enough for us to apply Paul's teaching to our own lives, and even in a slightly broader way: as guidance for discerning and understanding how we can serve God's people with our own particular gifts.

But I have to wonder about moments in my own life in which I just might have allowed the call to discern my gifts to become a distracting temptation. How could this be? Well, actually, pretty easily. For as I'm busy looking inward, a lonely elderly neighbor, an ailing coworker, a family member suffering silently under my very own roof are all waiting. No specialized gifts or talents required. Only love, poured out from the heart of Christ.

Jesus, form me in your gift of sacrificial love, above all.

Amy Welborn

What Does It Mean for Us?

Whoever remains in love remains in God and God in him.

1 John 4:16

We have recently celebrated Christmas and Epiphany. Very big events! But where do they connect with our lives? John shows where. When we acknowledge Jesus as God's son, John tells us, God gives us his Spirit. By his Spirit, we are able to love one another. Loving one another expresses the presence of God in us and among us. So there is the simple—and powerful—connection between Jesus' coming into the world and our small lives: By coming, he has empowered us to love; that love is his life within us.

If we let God's love have its way in us, John declares, it will come to "perfection among us" (verse 17). It will straighten out everything crooked in us; it will heal our hearts and bring us joy.

If Jesus' coming had not made it possible for us to love, what good would it have done for us that he was born in a stable and honored by magi? But he has done this for us. And so "we have come to know...the love God has for us" (verse 16).

Kevin Perrotta

LIVING WITH CHANGE

See, I am doing something new!
Now it springs forth, do you not perceive it? Isaiah 43:19

God's saving action as summed up in the Isaiah story continues to be repeated throughout our lives. We are constantly being delivered from death to life if we are willing to cooperate. I think of people like my friend who lost his job and began a successful business and my now deceased mother who found wonderful new friendships when her health forced her out of her beloved home and into assisted living.

Change, especially when it is thrust upon us rather than chosen, is rarely welcomed. We may feel disoriented, anxious and angry and resist the very things that will eventually prove to be life-giving. Worst of all, we so desperately want to hold on to the way things used to be that we entirely miss the gifts to be found in the present moment.

Saving God, give us eyes to see the wonder of your faithfulness.

Terri Mifek

JANUARY 24

FACING GOD

Hide not your face from me in the day of my distress.

Psalm 102:3

We seem to have some ambivalence about the face of God. On the one hand, we want the assurance of knowing God is out there; on the other hand, we may not want to pay the price, for the ancients believed that one could not see the face of God and live (Judges 13:22).

And it's not just an old-fashioned belief. We Christians have a classic picture of the face of God in Christ crucified, but he is not always easy to look upon, especially when we remember that we have been called to take up our own crosses and follow him. To the extent that we do, we will end up sharing that cross with him.

In the inevitable sufferings of our struggles to love and in all our human frailties, we will face the cross. Will we also see the face of God there, or will we be too afraid to look?

Lord, give me the courage to look upon your face that I may see your compassion and mercy.

Mark Neilsen

Supporting What Is Good

You always have the poor with you, but you do not always have me. John 12:8

Down through the centuries, this saying of Jesus has been used many times to justify everything from disregarding the needs of the poor and disadvantaged to not providing food for the hungry. This, of course, was not what Jesus meant.

He was not saying that there is no use in helping the poor and feeding the hungry, but that using money for seemingly "useless" purposes is valid too. Expanding on Jesus' meaning, we may say that while the poor and the hungry deserve our assistance, it's good also to help build a beautiful new church, support a music program, erect a monument to a good person or help construct bicycle paths as a way to cultivate a healthy, natural environment. Jesus' point may be that there are values of a spiritual or personal nature that are just as real as those of a physical and material nature, and they all deserve our support.

Lord Jesus, help me to support all that is good and true in the world.

Mitch Finley

A Home Fit for God

> I will not enter the house I live in,
>   nor lie on the couch where I sleep;
> I will give my eyes no sleep, my eyelids no rest,
>   Till I find a place for the LORD... Psalm 132:3-5

Artists, writers, musicians, all who wrestle with ashes of inspiration, often go hours, days, even longer without tending to the basic needs of eating and sleeping. There's a sense that, when one is possessed by the spark of creativity, one dare not rest, one dare not interrupt the creative process for fear that a visionary moment will be lost forever.

David was a psalmist with exactly such a single-minded vision. In his case, however, it wasn't only artistic inspiration that kept him from sleeping. He was possessed by his vision of building a home for God and his desire not to rest in his own house until he had built a fitting place for God to be at home.

Loving God, as I go through my everyday living, may you find a home and be at home in me.

Sr. Chris Koellhoffer, I.H.M.

Ancient Error, Modern Problem

The king made two calves of gold... 1 Kings 12:28

Why Jeroboam made two gold statues of calves and why the statues were not an acceptable part of worship of the Lord—well, those questions would take us deep into ancient Near Eastern history and Old Testament theology. But even without wrestling with such questions, it's obvious that the calf statues were bad because they distorted people's view of God. The calves, then, represent an issue that each of us face: Is my personal mental image of God correct and true? Or is my picture of God distorted by my childhood experiences, my fears, my desires, my sins? More than likely, there are unrecognized golden calves in all our minds.

What can one do about such an elusive problem? Here are three suggestions. First, we can ask the Holy Spirit—the Spirit of truth—to purify our minds. Second, we can read the gospels to get to know Jesus. He is the perfect image of God. Third, we can pay attention to the prayers of the liturgy. The Church's words to God reflect a deep understanding of who God really is.

Kevin Perrotta

SPIRITUAL GARDENING

This is how it is with the kingdom of God; it is as if a man were to scatter seed on the land and would sleep and rise night and day and the seed would sprout and grow, he knows not how. Mark 4:26-27

Next to my desk at work is posted a Zen proverb that offers an even more passive version of Jesus' words: "Sit quietly, doing nothing, spring comes and the grass grows by itself." For some folks, this invitation to inertia could be deadly, but for a very task-oriented (some might say obsessed) person like myself, I need both reminders to help me realize that my role in kingdom building is simply to scatter seeds.

This gospel message assures me that God really does have the rest covered. However, instead of fussing about how fast things are growing and whose plants are bigger, I'd best examine what kinds of seeds I choose to scatter, when and where I choose to plant these seeds and in what kind of soil. I don't need time-lapse photography to show me just how slowly and imperceptibly spiritual growth happens. I just have to leave it to my Master Gardener.

Claire J. King

We Are Not Alone

Jesus was in the stern, asleep... Mark 4:38

Perhaps most of us have never lived through a storm at sea such as the one Mark describes. I suspect, though, that many of us can name and identify with the emotions of that wild, terrifying ride.

Whether the "storm at sea" comes from lying awake at night in fear of what our children's lives may be, struggling with the abrupt loss of a job we once thought secure, facing the news of physical or mental diminishment, or grieving a broken relationship, all carry the terror of feeling alone and helpless.

This gospel story reminds us that, as the waves rise and surge, Jesus is still in the boat with us. He may not be visible, his presence may not be apparent, but he will not abandon us, no matter what. This same Jesus who invites us into the boat will accompany us and surround us with his love through all the storms of life.

Sr. Chris Koellhoffer, I.H.M.

LOVE IS PATIENT

Love is patient, love is kind. 1 Corinthians 13:4

Certainly patience is a virtue. Patience is a mark of good character. But why, precisely, must love be patient?

Love is patient, of course, because God is love, and how patient God is with you and me!

I think about all the missteps in my life, the habits that have built up walls between me and God and between me and others whom God has sent into my life. I think about the times I have listened to every other voice out there but God's.

But God still loves, unfailingly. And the love that is poured out for me—quite concretely in the loving, patient sacrifice of Jesus—where is it to go? To others, in love. Patient, forgiving, merciful love.

Loving God, you are so patient with me. Thank you. Help me love others as you love me.

Amy Welborn

Pray for Wisdom

Give your servant, therefore, an understanding heart to judge your people and to distinguish right from wrong. 1 Kings 3:9

I am always edified when I read the prayer of the young King Solomon, requesting from God the gift he wanted more than any other. He asked for an understanding heart and the ability to know right from wrong. The Lord said he could have asked for riches, power or revenge on his enemies, but instead he asked for wisdom. Solomon wanted wisdom to help others. His example could improve our modern-day conduct, which is so often driven by excessive greed and narrow-minded selfishness. We would do well each day to pray for wisdom—not just knowledge but wisdom. Knowledge can accomplish much good, but it can also be used to harm and destroy. Wisdom lives not only in the intellect but in the heart. Wisdom will never do wrong. Wisdom is precious, and the more we have, the better the world will be.

Fr. James McKarns

Wisdom: More Than Words

The mouth of the just man tells of wisdom... Psalm 37:30

Scholars tell us that language is a gift. It comes to us at a very early age, through others. In some ways, and for most children, it is as natural as breathing. If all goes well, single words soon flower into patterns of sentences, paragraphs and, hopefully, eloquence. The process takes time and patience. Speaking is God's gift bestowed on us through others.

Wisdom is also a gift and, like language, is given us by God. Through openness to the Spirit, we learn the ways of prayer, the pathways of hope and the boundlessness of love.

Wisdom may blossom into words, but it may also be known through the reverence that is silence or waiting or patience. It may be experienced through a deep-hearted listening and knowing that God, too, may have his moments of quiet when something more than words is discerned. God spoke, and a universe burst into being.

Fr. James Stephen Behrens, O.C.S.O.

THE 'YES' IN 'NOT RIGHT NOW'

He said to her, "Let the children be fed first. For it is not right to take the food of the children and throw it to the dogs." She replied and said to him, "Lord, even the dogs under the table eat the children's scraps." Mark 7:27-28

"Not today. Maybe another time." We've all heard words like these when we've asked a non-churchgoing relative or friend to accompany us to Mass. And we generally don't ask again; who wants to be a pest?

But the Syrophoenician woman didn't give up. The stakes were high; a demon possessed her daughter. She countered respectfully when Jesus tried to put her off. When she got home, the demon was gone.

Does "yes" or "no" lie behind a polite refusal? It's hard to know. But when it's a matter of faith, God calls on us to ask again—and again. After all, the stakes couldn't be higher.

Lord, give me the wisdom to get to "yes" as I strive to lead souls to your kingdom.

Melanie Rigney

CALLED BY NAME

No longer shall you be called Abram; your name shall be Abraham, for I am making you the father of a host of nations.

Genesis 17:5

Naming holds such power. We humans have classified names for flowers, trees, birds, insects. We name our pets and sometimes even inanimate objects like toys or cars. When we're about to welcome a child into the world, we spend long hours consulting baby books, mulling over possibilities of girls' or boys' names, exploring our ancestry for connections to family, culture or heritage.

When God changes Abram's name to "Abraham," the naming signifies a gift: Abraham is being called to a new way of life, a new role as the "father" of many nations, with all the responsibilities and challenges that implies. Abraham is charged with growing into the very definition of his name and living into the fullness of its meaning.

Today, reflect on the name you received in baptism. Recall any stories your ancestors may have shared with you about it, and ask: through my naming in baptism, what is God calling me to live into?

Sr. Chris Koellhoffer, I.H.M.

'Getting Through February'

> Wisdom instructs her children…
>   and at first she puts him to the test…
>   Then she comes back to bring him happiness
>   and reveal her secrets to him. Sirach 4:11, 17, 18

This ancient passage resonates deeply with the life I have experienced through many decades and stages. The secrets of wisdom are not easily accessible. Trials and difficulties, described here as the "discipline" of Wisdom's instruction, are necessary before her secrets are revealed. We grow into wisdom in times that are like winter in our souls.

I once moved from Florida to Notre Dame University in Indiana. The first winter there absolutely stunned me: the sub-zero weather, the days, even weeks, without sun. I heard an expression I have never forgotten: "Getting through February." A wisdom secret of Indiana natives was how to hold on through winter. It seemed to me that the way they did it was with lighthearted kindness. People would check on each other. Someone brought over a pot of stew. Everyone shared jokes. Neighbors formed snow-shoveling teams. There was even a February party.

Patricia Livingston

God Among Us

My dwelling shall be with them. Ezekiel 37:27

So much of our worldview is shaped by where and with whom we live. Growing up in a rural area, my family and I have all come away with a sense of kinship with the created world. Having spent much of my adult life in urban ministries, I have an equally deep appreciation for the resiliency and street smarts that characterize the children of our cities. We are forever marked by the remembrance of home.

Ezekiel's life was shaped by the experience of exile in Babylon during the period before and after the fall of Jerusalem. To be an exile, to be kept far from the familiar and the cherished, must have made Ezekiel live with longing for the kingdom God described: People gathered back from where they were scattered. Returned to the land they loved. Home. And most comforting of all, God's promise, "My dwelling shall be with them."

This promise is also for us and for all time: God will live here with us. Right now, right where we are. Home.

Sr. Chris Koellhoffer, I.H.M.

A Lot of Fish to Leave Behind

They left everything and followed him. Luke 5:11

Peter had been following Jesus for a while before Jesus gave him a miraculous catch of fish, and Peter left everything to follow him. So in a way, it was a second conversion for Peter. And perhaps that makes the incident a model for you and me of the possibility of our coming to a deeper conversion to Jesus.

If so, what's the message? Hope Jesus will work a miracle before our eyes too—and in the meantime, just go on living as we've been living? That sounds a little too easy. Is the message that we should, right now, give up everything to follow Jesus? But where does he want us to go?

I suggest that Luke offers his account for reflection and prayer. Peter's experience of Jesus spurs us to ask where we have experienced Jesus at work in our lives and in the lives of others. If I think quietly about that, do I hear Jesus saying something to me about where he wants me to follow him? And do I see a boatload of fish holding me back?

Kevin Perrotta

How Awesome Is Our God

O Lord, our Lord,
   how glorious is your name over all the earth! Psalm 8:2

When I gave my five-year-old grandnephew a cookie, he took it into his hand and exclaimed, "Awesome!" I had to smile, for I have long maintained that the word "awesome" is overused today—as a quick response to almost anything we deem "nice." But in today's psalm, the word "awesome" would be entirely appropriate.

When we behold creation, what other response can we have except how awesome God must be? Pay close attention to anything—a tiny ant, a graceful deer, a flowering forsythia, the gradual fading of day into night—and what better response than, "Awesome!"

Today might be a good day to really notice at least one aspect of God's incredible creation—a particular tree, the stars, the steady beating of our heart—and give thanks to our awesome God.

Sr. Melannie Svoboda, S.N.D.

DON'T BE AFRAID
OF THE DARK

Then Solomon said, "The Lord intends to dwell in the dark cloud." 1 Kings 8:12

Living faith in the light is lovely. We join hands and marvel at the miracles and joy found in community ministries and in public celebrations of baptism, marriage and the Eucharist.

But God also is there in the dark cloud, as Solomon noted when the ark of the covenant was brought to the new temple. Darkness, St. John of the Cross wrote, "signifies the obscurity of faith with which the divinity is clothed while communicating itself to the soul."

In a quietly profound way, living faith in the darkness of crisis and struggle and uncertainty can be lovely as well, for what we learn while we're there moves us closer to the light.

Lord, help me to appreciate the darkness as you lead me to the light.

Melanie Rigney

WE ALL NEED REASSURANCE

Come, have breakfast. John 21:12

Breakfast with Jesus over a charcoal fire at a beach on the Sea of Tiberias. Sounds like the start of a good day.

For some strange reason, the apostles have gone back to their old profession of fishing. They are out on the water all night and have nothing to show for it. As they row in, someone beckons from the shore. He calls them "children." He inquires about the fishing. It's not good, they reply. He tells them to drop a net. Presto! The net is filled with fish. As they pull the net ashore, they see it is Jesus who has called to them. He has a fire ready to cook the fish, and he intends to serve these apostles, whom he has chosen to be fishers of souls.

This meeting after the resurrection is a lot more than breakfast. It is Jesus assuring his unsteady apostles—and us—that without God, our nets will be empty; with God, they will be filled, and all things are possible. We all need a little reassurance from time to time.

Paul Pennick

LEARNING TO LISTEN

Go into the whole world and proclaim the gospel to every creature. Mark 16:15

Some of the best advice given to me over the years was the importance of listening and listening well. I may not have heeded it right away. It took time for me to realize the value of those few words of kind advice. In terms of proclaiming the gospel, if whatever I may have preached or written over the years has helped others to listen better, I am glad about that.

Practicing the Good News is partly telling and partly listening. A person who listens well teaches well. He or she may never give a formal homily or take to any kind of a pulpit. But those who know such people are encountering a rather unique way of spreading the gospel. Our words are only as good as we have learned to listen, so that when we do speak, we have something of worth to say.

Fr. James Stephen Behrens, O.C.S.O.

Recycling Our Resources

> Those who owned property or houses would sell them, bring the proceeds of the sale, and put them at the feet of the apostles, and they were distributed to each according to need. Acts 4:34-35

Talk of redistribution of tangible wealth can make us uncomfortable. We tell ourselves that large-scale attempts to do it in the modern world have failed, primarily because those responsible were mere mortals and looked out for themselves, not the greater good.

Perhaps there's another, more attainable lesson in this reading from Acts. What if "property" included the time to drive a neighbor to the doctor or a donation of accounting skills to a parish ministry? What if bringing the proceeds of the sale included donating an unexpected bonus to a homeless shelter or enlightening friends about community service opportunities?

The early Christian community pooled their physical resources because they thought the Second Coming was at hand. They were wrong. If we pool our time, talent and treasure to help others because we burn to grow closer to Christ, can that be wrong?

Lord, help us to slow down and put our treasures at your feet.

Melanie Rigney

GETTING BACK TO THE ESSENTIALS

For God did not send his Son into the world to condemn the world... John 3:17

This gospel reading contains one of the most well-known of all the passages in the New Testament: John 3:16. Occasionally in public areas, committed Christians will hold up signs with this citation. Others have put this Scripture reference on their cars' license plates or on walls in their homes.

These signs are meant to summarize, in one simple sentence, the gospel message. I think they have made a good choice. This is truly a core message of the New Testament: God sent his Son to us because he loves us and wants us to be saved. His offer to us, in Jesus, is not one of punishment. Rather, he offers us life.

Sometimes we make the message of salvation too complicated or too negative. From time to time, it is good to get back to the essentials. John 3:16 summarizes this Good News for us: "For God so loved the world that he gave his only Son, so that everyone who believes in him might not perish but might have eternal life." We do well to let these simple yet profound words resonate in our hearts.

Msgr. Stephen J. Rossetti

ACTING WISELY

> If you are the Son of God, throw yourself down from here, for it is written: "He will command his angels concerning you, to guard you..." Luke 4:9-10

At first glance, this suggestion might seem to make sense. If people saw a miracle like this, wouldn't they automatically follow Jesus? But Jesus wisely dismisses the devil's suggestion because this quick, ashy miracle would not have helped to form bonds of love between Jesus and his followers.

Lasting relationships only develop with time. And they have to be based on love. It was only through his death and resurrection that Jesus could reveal the depths of his love. The cross is the ultimate sign of what God was willing to endure for us. Nothing else can take its place.

Jesus, you showed your wisdom by dismissing the devil's suggestions. Give me your wisdom so I may do the same.

Fr. Kenneth Grabner, C.S.C.

HEARING TO OBEY

We must obey God rather than men. Acts 5:29

Peter says these words to the Sanhedrin in Jerusalem. It causes great consternation among these Jewish judicial and religious leaders, who contemplate putting Peter and all the new Christians to death.

Jesus was always more interested in the kingdom of God than the kingdoms of this world. We think of the early disciples heroically facing down death and imprisonment as they deliver the Good News. And while heroic confrontations make for a compelling Bible story, it is probably not a likely scenario for us.

Our conflicts will most likely occur in the quiet of a troubled heart, trying to sort out God's voice from the heavy static that surrounds us. It is never easy to do this. There are so many opportunities to become diverted. And there are times when we refuse to even listen because we are not heroes. We are frail human souls sorely in need of God's help.

Dear Lord, help me recognize your voice and obey your laws.

Paul Pennick

Called to Evangelize

Go into the whole world and proclaim the gospel to every creature. Mark 16:15

Today, people tend to think of religion as a private affair and not to "impose" one's beliefs on others. As I heard it said recently in response to a street evangelizer, "That may be your truth, but it's not my truth. We all have our own truths." But embedded in the very nature of our Christian faith is a call to evangelize. Why? Because there is salvation in no other name but the name of Jesus, as the Scriptures tell us. Jesus challenged people to choose this Way and this Life. The challenge is no less urgent today.

These are unpopular ideas in our relativistic world. But Christianity can be a very unpopular religion. St. Mark, often depicted by a lion, was said to have preached the gospel in North Africa. There he was martyred. May God give us the courage of this Lion to preach the gospel, even when it comes at great cost.

Msgr. Stephen J. Rossetti

OUR WORDS MEAN SOMETHING

> They instigated some men to say, "We have heard him speaking blasphemous words against Moses and God." They stirred up the people, the elders, and the scribes, accosted him, seized him, and brought him before the Sanhedrin.
>
> Acts 6:11-12

The writer of Acts goes on to recount how gossip and libel ultimately led to the murder of Stephen, a faith-filled assistant to the apostles. It is a sharp reminder of how much damage otherwise good people can do by passing along opinions as "facts" and allowing the scurrilous bad-mouthing of others to go unchallenged. Psychologists call this "relational aggression": no physical violence is done, but the aim is to threaten, destroy or, at the very least, throw a wedge in people's good, working relationships with others.

This week I want to place a stone on my desk at work and one on my kitchen table as a reminder of the consequences my speech or my silence can have on the good name of others.

Holy Spirit, today may my words or my silence only be loving, only be true.

Claire J. King

FAITH WITHOUT SIGNS

[Jesus] ordered them not to tell anyone. But the more he ordered them not to, the more they proclaimed it. Mark 7:36

So many of Jesus' miracles took place in very public places: the marriage feast at Cana, the loaves and fishes, the raising of Lazarus. Witnesses were everywhere; people marveled at his powers of healing. Yet here in Sidon he takes a deaf man with a speech impediment aside and heals him. He asks the crowd not to talk about this miracle. Why does he want to keep this one quiet? Could it be that Jesus wants us to concentrate on things other than miracles?

While his powers of healing are incredible and amazing, they are not central to his message of love, hope, forgiveness, mercy, compassion. When Jesus is not physically present, all that is left is belief. Our faith is more than miracles and healing. Faith is belief without signs. Faith, as Jean-Pierre de Caussade writes, "grasps the truth without seeing it."

Paul Pennick

Teach Children, Trust God

> Whoever obeys and teaches these commandments will be called greatest in the kingdom of heaven. Matthew 5:19

Passing on the faith has so many different facets. You want to be able to share an important part of your life with your children. You want them to be happy, and if anything is essential to happiness, it is having a sense of your place in the world. You want them to be assured of salvation through Jesus Christ.

But "teaching" is not browbeating or haranguing or needling. Children need to be taught, and then they need to grow up and choose for themselves. Surely, parents of adults remember teaching their children how much God loves them, how the Holy Spirit will never abandon them, how Jesus came to bring all of us life to the full. May we remember what we have taught and been taught, and take comfort in the knowledge of God's great love for us.

Lord, may the love between parents and children grow and bear fruit in faithfulness—in all of us.

Mark Neilsen

AN OUTWARD SIGN OF OUR FAITH

**A clean heart create for me, O God,
and a steadfast spirit renew within me.** Psalm 51:12

Ash Wednesday, in all its solemnity and reverence, is one of my favorite religious days. I love the humble act of repentance, the cross formed by ashes across my forehead reminding me that without Christ, I am nothing more than ashes. As I emerge from the quiet of Mass into the glare of my church parking lot, I imagine the dusty gray cross looks even bolder in the outside light.

It remains on my forehead for the remainder of the day. People with similar markings catch my eye and smile. Others, with barren foreheads, stare and wonder. It catches my own attention if I glimpse my reflection in a mirror or window. It is a day to reflect inward, certainly, in preparation of the Lenten journey ahead. But it is also a day to express our faith outwardly, to remind the world that each of us must carry our cross with compassion and courage—in the image of our Savior.

Kristin Armstrong

BEING ATTENTIVE TO THE PAUSES

This is the will of the one who sent me, that I should not lose anything of what he gave me, but that I should raise it [on] the last day. John 6:39

The novelist Henry James' advice to new writers was to try to be a person "upon whom nothing was lost." I take that advice to heart, not just as a sometime writer, but as a human being and a follower of Jesus. The gospels are filled with rich examples of Jesus so fully present to all that the Father unfolded before him in his daily life as a human being on this earth, each telling the story of the Son of God fully alive in the human experience. Jesus never skips a beat. He embraces each person he encounters as an unrepeatable individual, sees each creature and grain of wheat as they are and more, as a metaphor for the kingdom's coming, for the moment-by-moment revelation of the Word of God alive in our world.

Let's not lose a minute today, not a precious second in frenetic activity, but instead be deeply attentive during the pauses between each appointment, each phone call, each meeting, each task, and lift up all our endeavors to God.

Claire J. King

ACTING ON AN IMPULSE

> As they traveled along the road they came to some water, and the eunuch said, "Look, there is water. What is to prevent my being baptized?" Acts 8:36

What, indeed, prevents me? Not from being baptized (since that happened long ago), but from really opening myself to the grace of that baptism and growing in my faith?

Pride? Fear of losing some part of my life I believe is essential? A hesitancy to give up control? A fear of what others might say or think? Claims that I'm too busy, that I'm fine just as I am?

The Ethiopian eunuch was moved by the Spirit. He didn't push that nudge aside, ignore it or try to argue it away. I have to wonder about the nudges I have felt today. What is to prevent me from listening and acting on them?

Lord, break down the obstacles I've put up to your presence.

Amy Welborn

The Cornerstone of Life

The stone which the builders rejected has become the cornerstone. Psalm 118:22

How could a stone be used as the cornerstone after the builders had decided it wouldn't work? A friend who makes his living as a builder helped me find the answer: The builder decides which stones will work in terms of size, color and placement. But even if the builder has rejected a certain stone, the stonemason can help the builder to reassess that decision. The decision to use something previously rejected may come about because the stone's particular shape or color will offer the building a unique strength and/or beauty beyond the typical.

Charismatic and powerful, Jesus embodied a new way of relating to God and to others beyond what people had ever seen. Rejected by the "business as usual" religion of the Pharisees and scribes, Jesus was "reassessed" by anyone who sought the beautiful life Jesus promised: personal nearness to God and compassionate love for others. He became the cornerstone that could hold a life and a community together.

Fr. James Krings

A Good Choice

You are Peter, and upon this rock I will build my church...

Matthew 16:18

Jesus picked Peter for a reason. The New Testament tells us Peter was every bit as awed as you or me. Could we have spent three years with Jesus, a close companion, a devoted disciple, and then, even after we were warned, publicly deny we ever knew him? Of course, we could. We are frail humans, and we will take every opportunity to save ourselves.

Peter gives us hope. He embodies all our faults and all our dreams of saintliness. Despite—or perhaps because of—his humanness, Peter is chosen by Jesus to establish his Church here on earth. He did not pick an elder in the temple, an expert on the Torah, a Scribe or Pharisee. Instead, he picked a simple fisherman, someone who could easily mix among other ordinary people, someone who could speak about Jesus in ways everyday people might understand. It was the perfect choice.

Paul Pennick

TURNING MY FACE TO GOD

> But they obeyed not, nor did they pay heed. They walked in the hardness of their evil hearts and turned their backs, not their faces, to me. Jeremiah 7:24

I consider myself to be a person of faith in most areas of my life. I go to church. I donate things I don't use to St. Vincent de Paul Society. If a cashier gives me too much change, I give back the extra. Sometimes I take muffins to my neighbors. But there are parts of my life I don't want to look at very closely. I'm hoping God won't notice.

God doesn't insist that we be perfect. But the areas that we least want to change are the very ones in which we can experience the most grace. God wants to touch all the wounds in our lives. God wants to make us whole. And God is the only one who can.

Where is the darkness in your life? Maybe there is a person you feel you can never forgive. Maybe you feel superior to somebody. Maybe there is a pleasure you are too attached to. You know what it is. God knows too. Let God transform you.

God, help me turn my face to you.

Karla Manternach

A Path Out of Darkness

I came into the world as light, so that everyone who believes in me might not remain in darkness. John 12:46

The church at my parish has several mercury vapor lights. When there is a power outage, they go out like all the others. However, when the power returns, the mercury lights only gradually reach full brightness, compared to the other lights that go on immediately.

For me, these lights have come to symbolize one way the light of Christ shines in the world. I have been blessed personally, and I have seen Christ's brilliant light in others too. Then, like a finger snap, there is the darkness of personal illness, tragic loss, crushing evil. The darkness descends like a spiritual power outage that cannot be restored by any quick fix.

Instead, like a mercury vapor light, faith sparks again and grows gradually, the light of Christ leading us, in time, out of the darkness.

Dear Jesus, if I feel darkness today, shine your light in the crevices of my soul where I most need you.

Fr. James Krings

Cherishing Jesus' Presence

Whoever loves me will keep my word, and my Father will love him, and we will come to him and make our dwelling with him.

John 14:23

The meaning of these familiar words of Jesus may seem fairly obvious. But there is a powerful message packed into just one sentence. Jesus says that if we love him we will "keep" his "word." But what does it mean to keep Jesus' word? Perhaps it means to hang on to and cherish Jesus' teachings. Or perhaps it means to cultivate Jesus' teachings in one's heart. Maybe it means both. Probably it means both.

So if we love the Lord Jesus and cherish and cultivate his teachings in our heart, our loving Father in heaven will love us to the point that both he and the Lord Jesus will come to us, be with us and actually take up residence with us.

Lord Jesus, help me to act on your word and cherish your presence.

Mitch Finley

Fasting for Others

This, rather, is the fasting that I wish:
    releasing those bound unjustly...
Sharing your bread with the hungry...
Clothing the naked when you see them... Isaiah 58:6-7

Isaiah reminds us that religious people must also be people of justice. Religious practices like fasting are meant to support and nourish concrete acts of love. And our own sins are somehow healed when we reach out to others in compassion. These words are sobering. They imply that my Lenten practices are not a private affair between God and me. As the old proverb says, "Be not simply good; be good for something."

How am I working to build a more just world—starting in my own home, workplace, parish and neighborhood? With whom am I sharing my "bread"—whether that bread is food, money, time, talents or attention? Who am I helping to free from bondage—the bondage of addiction, ignorance, poverty, sickness, loneliness, poor self-esteem?

God of love, may my Lenten practices support my endeavors to make this world a better place.

Sr. Melannie Svoboda, S.N.D.

Finding God

...so that people might seek God, even perhaps grope for him
and find him, though indeed he is not far from any one of us.

Acts 17:27

Many years ago as a member of a young adult faith group, I went
on my first and only spelunking adventure in an ancient cave
beneath the Ozark hills of southern Missouri. I remember that at
one point, we all turned off our flashlights and experienced total,
utter darkness. I literally could not see my hand in front of my face,
and for a terrifying moment, I imagined what it would be like to
have to grope my way out of the cave, inch by inch, not knowing if
I would ever see the light of day again.

In our journeys of faith, we sometimes experience "dark nights
of the soul" when God seems nowhere to be found, and darkness
masks any sense of light, hope or joy. But the mystery and majesty
of our relationship with Christ is that he is, in fact, always near,
standing close by and awaiting our hands to reach out to him in
prayer, yearning for his touch.

Jesus, see me in the darkness. Show me your light.

Steve Givens

March 1

THE WAY TO FAST

**Would that today you might fast
so as to make your voice heard on high!** Isaiah 58:4

What does a fast day mean to you? We all know about "no meat on Fridays," but Isaiah reminds us that genuine fasting involves more than grabbing a fish filet and continuing on our day. Fasting, rightly undertaken, will make us more aware of our blessings and turn our minds toward God. At that point, our sacrifices will open our hearts to the needs of other people and help create justice in the world.

It's easy to cruise through life, take care of ourselves and our own pursuits, and forget the people around us. But loving relationships are built on time, attention and sharing what we have. This Lent, let us think of fasting not as just another achievement of our own, but as a step toward greater awareness of what other people need.

Lord, may I fast so as to make my voice heard on high today.

Julia DiSalvo

In God's Time...

When they had gathered together they asked him, "Lord, are you at this time going to restore the kingdom to Israel?"

Acts 1:6

The disciples could not let go of a dream that was so deep in their hearts: Surely the Christ would restore the kingdom of Israel! After all that had happened, God could not possibly leave this task undone, could he?

Like the disciples, we all have our own dreams for what God must surely want to accomplish in the world: an end to poverty, to abortion, to violence and to the long list of plagues and injustices that we can so easily catalog. And maybe someday God will take care of every last one of those things we wish he would do right now.

Jesus doesn't tell the disciples they are wrong to wish for the kingdom of Israel, only that God's timing is not theirs to know. We can keep our hopes and dreams alive only if we are willing to deepen our trust in the rightness of God's plan, including its timing.

Gracious God, set us free from all the limits we want to put on your action in the world.

Mark Neilsen

March 3

Tried and True

No one has ever seen God. Yet, if we love one another, God remains in us, and his love is brought to perfection in us.

1 John 4:12

When John, the beloved apostle, was advanced in age, he preached a message consisting of only five words: "Little children, love one another." He had distilled the wisdom of his many years of Christian living into this brief message. Most likely, John was simply restating the words of Jesus, who had told the crowds they needed to become like little children to enter the kingdom of heaven. It is easy to see the divine love and beauty of God in the face, eyes and trusting ways of a little child.

To improve our love for one another and strengthen the presence of God within us, we don't need to find new and exotic religious practices. We need only to remember that innocent, trusting love we had as children and then replicate that in our adult lives.

Fr. James McKarns

What Is Your Legacy?

Well for the man who is gracious and lends,
   who conducts his affairs with justice.
He shall never be moved;
   the just man shall be in everlasting remembrance.

Psalm 112:5-6

You can prove the truth of these words from your own experience. Do you remember Martin Luther King, Jr.? He is revered even now, years after his courageous fight for justice. And you probably remember Mother Teresa. Her spirited care for the poor continues to inspire us. The memories of these two people will be treasured because they lived their lives for others.

What about you? How will you be remembered by your family, your friends and the people you work with? I often think about a religious brother who responded enthusiastically to the many financial appeals that came his way, even though his meager monthly allowance barely provided for his own needs. People who are generous to others often live in other people's memories. They are a gift to us all.

Lord, through your help, may I be remembered among those who conduct their affairs with justice.

Fr. Kenneth E. Grabner, C.S.C.

SURRENDERING TO GOD

Repay to Caesar what belongs to Caesar and to God what belongs to God. Mark 12:17

Throughout the gospels, Jesus gets hit with questions, designed sometimes to justify the questioner, sometimes to catch Jesus in a faulty answer. But never do these questions manage to get the best of him. Instead, he always raises the discussion to a new level.

Consider the matter of whether or not to pay taxes. On the one hand, not to pay would be a civic violation; on the other hand, to pay would be a collaboration with the enemy. Jesus, uninterested in such a limited framework, turns to the issue of "what belongs to God." Much more important than mere taxation, this is the heart of the matter of our allegiance.

We all would like Jesus to side with us on secular and religious issues of the day, but he would very likely move us beyond our either/or questions to consider the kingdom that God desires to bring into being. Seek that kingdom first, he might say, and all these other issues will be resolved as well.

Lord, help us to give up trying to justify ourselves and instead surrender our hearts to you.

Mark Neilsen

A VISION OF HEAVEN

When they rise from the dead, they neither marry nor are given in marriage, but they are like the angels in heaven.

Mark 12:25

To misunderstand the resurrection as the Sadducees did would be unfortunate. But even today, people occasionally have strange ideas about what their resurrected life will be like. Some imagine they will be in a heavenly choir, constantly singing the praises of God. Others imagine they will be resting without end as they float on a bank of clouds. What a prescription for boredom! God did not create us to be bored. He created us to be fully alive!

When we resurrect into our new life, our relationship with God will be transformed. We will love God passionately. We will experience his unconditional love enthusiastically. We will love and admire his entire creation unreservedly. Our joy will be overflowing, and nothing will be able to take our joy away. That is God's plan for us.

Lord, thank you for the gift of life that continues to grow into ever deeper levels of fulfillment.

Fr. Kenneth E. Grabner, C.S.C.

Counting on God's Touch

The LORD keeps faith forever,
   secures justice for the oppressed,
   gives food to the hungry. Psalm 146:6-7

This consoling psalm is an inspiration for those times when life's difficulties knock at our door. When we feel lonely and weak, we can count on God's fidelity to uphold us. When we feel lost, we can trust in God's promise to guide us. When we are oppressed by our inability to love and forgive, we can believe in God's power to free us. God's love touches us at every moment. We have only to recognize it in our daily lives as we are strengthened by its power.

Lord, may my hope in you bring me peace, and may it give me the strength to become what you made me to be.

Fr. Kenneth E. Grabner, C.S.C.

'Where Is God?'

You must now know…that the Lord is God in the heavens above and on earth below, and that there is no other.

Deuteronomy 4:39

A friend told me her terrible difficulties. My heart went out to her. She looked at me quizzically: "Where's God?"

It's a common question of our age, and not a bad one. Where is God? We know where pain and suffering, anxiety and loneliness are. They can lead us to look for God, even if we don't know how or where to look. They're apparently everywhere, so where could God be hiding?

Deuteronomy points us on our search. The Israelites know where God is, Moses reminds them, because they know their own story. They can look back and can see how God has acted within and among them. By retelling the story in faith, they can learn to know God. If we look back at our lives, will we be able to see God? To see he's not only in heaven, but on earth, where the pain and suffering are?

Lord, teach me how you are on earth as in heaven.

Mary Marrocco

GOD IS OUR CHEERLEADER

Blessed be the God and Father of our Lord Jesus Christ, the Father of compassion and God of all encouragement, who encourages us in our every affliction, so that we may be able to encourage those who are in any affliction...

1 Corinthians 1:3-4

Of the many kinds of friends—the helper, the advisor, the confidant, the companion, the jester—the cheerleader is one of the most important. This is the friend who encourages us when we're down, overwhelmed or on the verge of giving up. This is the friend who says just the right words, pats us on the back, reminds us of our goodness and abilities, and then nudges us back onto the playing field of life.

According to St. Paul, all encouragement ultimately comes from God, so, in one way, we can say (respectfully, of course) that God is our greatest cheerleader. Today, let us thank God for all the cheerleaders in our lives. Also, let us ask ourselves: For whom might I become a cheerleader?

Encouraging God, thank you for all the ways you remind me of your love for me and encourage me to use my gifts in the game of life.

Sr. Melannie Svoboda, S.N.D.

DOING FOR OTHERS

Remember that you received what was good during your lifetime while Lazarus likewise received what was bad.

Luke 16:25

This parable of the rich man and the poor man, Lazarus, haunts me when I fail to reach out to others because of my self-absorption or disregard for their concerns. It's quite easy to see how the wealthy man ignored the pleas of Lazarus who was "covered with sores, who longed to satisfy his hunger with what fell from the rich man's table." I ask myself if I, living with comfort and plenty, can at least let go of what enriches me during six weeks of Lent. Can I fast from buying "stuff" and give the unspent money to those with less? Can I fast from clutching precious time to myself so I can be with others who long for someone to ease their loneliness or sorrow? There are countless "Lazaruses" in my life. This Lent I'll keep before me one thought: When I die, it will be the things I did not do that I will most regret.

Sr. Joyce Rupp, O.S.M.

A Party for the Unworthy

But now we must celebrate and rejoice... Luke 15:32

Embarrassing as it is to acknowledge this, I often feel like the Prodigal Son's older brother. I completely understand his sentiments. He was not able to rejoice over another's good fortune because he was focusing on whether the recipient of his father's love was truly deserving. He was also wallowing in his own imagined neglect: I've been faithful all these years, and no one even noticed. Poor me! This gospel offers marvelous material for prayer and reflection for each of us. Are we able to rejoice with another because of some good gift they've received whether it be a material gift, a promotion or new opportunity, an affirmation or reward? Or has our fountain of joy dried up because we are foundering in our own misery?

Look deep within your heart to see if there may be a bit of rejoicing you are withholding. Practice being glad because of another's good fortune.

Oh, most merciful One, teach me to throw a party for the unworthy, knowing that I may be the guest of honor.

Sr. Macrina Weiderkehr, O.S.B.

A Love That Can't Be Hidden

A city set on a mountain cannot be hidden. Matthew 5:14

Once I went uptown to meet a woman who was working for my company. We introduced ourselves, and I briefed her on the project. Afterwards, she told me she'd had an intense year following her husband's illness and death. She spoke about him, their marriage, their family. He'd been an architect. Her eyes were shining with grief, but also with the joy of who he was, including his faith in God.

She gestured behind her, where three tall new apartment buildings pointed to the sky. I'd noticed them before; they were artistic, beautiful, elegant. "That's my husband," she said. "He designed those buildings. If ever I lose sight of him, I only have to look up to see him shining."

It wasn't so much his skill as an architect that has remained with me. It's the light of love she showed me—not only their love of each other, but also their love of God. No bushel basket covered their lamp. Nor could this mountain city be hidden. Thank God.

Mary Marrocco

Righteousness: A Way of Life

Whoever obeys and teaches these commandments will be called greatest in the Kingdom of heaven. Matthew 5:19

No sooner does Jesus say this than he warns us not to consider ourselves great because of our righteousness. Righteousness is a good thing. It means that we think and act according to what is right, proper, true, just and fitting. But Jesus makes it clear that there are degrees of righteousness. The kind of righteousness he demands of his followers is more than a set of moral practices. It is the consistent expression of who we are. Righteousness is more than skin deep. It is the substance of our being. It is more than a notion. It is a way of life.

When we become a follower of Jesus, we do not simply believe. We become believers. It's as if our faith takes up permanent residence not only in our head and heart, but in every inch of our body. Even our hands, eyes, ears and feet become expressive parts of our whole believing person. In the end, it is Jesus himself who permeates all we are and do.

Jesus, increase my righteousness. Help all of me to follow you.

Sr. Melannie Svoboda, S.N.D.

BEARING FRUIT IN GOD'S NAME

I shall cultivate the ground around it and fertilize it; it may bear fruit in the future. If not you can cut it down. Luke 13:8-9

During Lent, we have a special opportunity to take a close look at whether we are living as disciples of Christ. Traditionally, we concentrate on those aspects of our lives that are interfering with our relationship with God. What sins, addictions or distractions keep you from following Jesus? What should you cut out of your life so that you may bear fruit? What ought you give up?

Another approach is to nourish and cultivate those areas of our lives that seem to be bearing fruit already. How are you already following Jesus? Do you feel close to him when you pray but don't make much time for it? Do you appreciate God's presence in nature but hardly ever go outside? Do you experience God's love when you spend time with family but find yourself spending more time working instead? How can you be more responsive to God?

Lord Jesus, help me to bear fruit in your name.

Karla Manternach

HEARTS FULL OF PRAYER

In praying, do not babble like the pagans, who think that they will be heard because of their many words. Matthew 6:7

Many words do not necessarily make good prayer. God hears your prayer not because of countless words but because of God's immense love. This truth is suggested by Jesus just before he teaches his disciples the Lord's Prayer.

Jesus is trying to open our hearts to recognize and value the spirit of prayer. He is indirectly saying, don't try to get heaven's attention by a lot of wordy prayers. As a child seeks the comfort of a loving parent, let your needs be known. Heaven leans down and listens to the prayer of a humble spirit. The One to whom you pray is holy; remember the hallowedness of God's name. Pray that the reign of God may surround you during your sojourn on earth. Yearn to do God's will. Lovingly anticipate your daily bread. Learn forgiveness. Learn to do good and not evil. Then your heart will be filled with the spirit of prayer.

Sr. Macrina Wiederkehr, O.S.B.

AWAY FROM THE COMFORT ZONE

The LORD said to Abram: "Go forth from the land of your kinsfolk and from your father's house to a land that I will show you." Genesis 12:1

I woke one morning with a powerful impulse to attend Mass as well as an equally strong desire to go back to sleep. Even more than the extra sleep, I wanted to avoid someone I suspected might attend that liturgy. In the end, I obeyed the inner nudge and went to Mass, where I immediately encountered the person I had successfully dodged for years.

I cannot put into words what happened that morning. How do you explain the mystery of forgiveness and reconciliation? I can say that finally letting go of the familiar feelings of anger, resentment and bitterness was extraordinarily freeing. When I learned that the person was moving out of state the next morning, I could only marvel at God's timing.

The Spirit continues to call us to move out of our comfort zone and into unfamiliar territory. Sometimes that involves a change in physical locations and at other times a change of heart.

Terri Mifek

HAIL, MARY...

Behold, you will conceive in your womb and bear a son, and you shall name him Jesus. Luke 1:31

When I read these first chapters of Luke's Gospel, I can't help but compare and contrast. On the one hand, there's Zechariah—John the Baptist's father—being struck mute in the temple, a grand, glorious place where only a few could encounter God in a hidden, privileged center.

And but a few miles north, a young, unknown woman in a backwater town held in contempt by anyone who bothered to think about it, was being touched by God. That moment was hidden, too, but would soon become anything but, as this young woman's son announced the Good News of salvation for all—and the temple veil was split as he announced this same Good News with the shedding of his blood.

Mary asked it, but I can't help but ask it in another sense. How can this be? Who are we that God loves us—all of us—so?

Hail Mary, full of grace, the Lord is with you.

Amy Welborn

Taking Up the Cross

If anyone wishes to come after me, he must deny himself and take up his cross daily and follow me. Luke 9:23

This verse stings like a slap in the face to our "immediate gratification society." Lent can be a large pill to swallow with a dry mouth for those of us who have grown accustomed to indulging our whims and seeking our own satisfaction.

Lent may be a difficult season, but like any challenge, it can also be the most worthwhile. We could all benefit from pausing long enough to distinguish between want and need. As we grow more comfortable sitting quietly with our longing without indulging it, we build spiritual character. We are able, with the help of the Holy Spirit, to learn how to deny ourselves. We can transform our weakness into something worthwhile. Our impatience can become steadfast endurance. Our gluttony can grow into gratitude. Our immediacy can be tempered by eternity. We can build our strength over these forty days. We can heft the load of our cross onto our shoulders and carry on.

Kristin Armstrong

RUNNING THE RACE

I have competed well; I have finished the race; I have kept the faith. 2 Timothy 4:7

Paul the apostle. Teresa of Avila. John of the Cross. Francis of Assisi. Elizabeth Seton. John Paul II. Mother Teresa. These individuals not only ran "the race," they believed that it was the only race worth running: the race laid out by the life, death and resurrection of Christ Jesus. It is marked out by his life and culminates in the mystery of his—and our—death and resurrection. On the way, we are accompanied by the Spirit and fed by the Lord's body in the Eucharist.

I was just reading a magazine in the waiting room of a doctor's office. A Christian musician was grieving the death of his child, and in his pain, he still believed. A politician's wife was forgiving her husband's affair in order to keep the family together. A lieutenant colonel was starting a scholarship fund for the children of soldiers slain in Iraq. They, too, are "running the race."

Whom do you know who is racing on the way of Christ Jesus? How can you support them? Urge them on? Applaud them?

Sr. Kathryn James Hermes, F.S.P.

Becoming Ourselves

She fell down before Jesus and told him the whole truth.

Mark 5:33

I can identify with the hemorrhaging woman's desire to be healed as well as her fear of doing what is necessary to bring that healing about. Knowing that she would make Jesus ceremonially unclean by touching him, I can't help but wonder what finally empowered her to risk his possible rejection and reach out for what she needed. What was it that she saw in the eyes of this holy man that liberated her from her fear and eventually allowed her to reveal her deepest secrets?

I suspect it is the same thing that we see in the eyes of those who so completely accept us that in their presence we are able to forget our shortcomings and wounds. What a relief it is to stop trying to prove how good we are and to know that it is safe to just be.

Lord, help us recognize you in all who see us through the eyes of love.

Terri Mifek

Being Faithful

**A clean heart create for me, O God,
and a steadfast spirit renew within me.** Psalm 51:12

With Lent and spring upon us, I'm reflecting on ants. Each morning, signs of their industrious work appear as little anthills on the walkway near my home. As the day progresses and foot traffic increases, the anthills are often trampled on, sometimes completely washed away by heavy rain. Yet no matter what happens to their work, the ants offer signs each morning that they've not given up, that they're renewing the efforts of the previous day.

We so often begin the season of Lent with intentions to enter into practices of penance, with promises to pray more deeply and more often, with high hopes for renewal. As the days move on, we may become aware of our failings to hold ourselves to our commitments. Yet what God calls us to is not perfection, but faithfulness, to trying our best to listen to God's voice in our everyday lives and to getting up each morning with a renewed heart.

Sr. Chris Koellhoffer, I.H.M.

Truly Seeing Jesus and Others

A prophet is not without honor except…among his own kin.

Mark 6:4

We do not always "see" the people around us, especially if they are well known to us. We have set in cement our ideas about these familiar faces, and we tend to filter out any information that contradicts it. The patterns are set. And, thus, we do not give others a chance to change or to surprise us.

The people in Jesus' town knew him, or at least they thought they did. Jesus was believed to be the son of the carpenter. Mary was his mother; they knew his relatives. Their ideas about him were fixed. Not surprisingly, they were among the ones who had the most difficulty believing in him.

Could we try, this day, to see those familiar faces around us with a mind free of old labels? Could we let go of the mental constraints we place on others? If we are able to do so, maybe those closest to us will surprise us. They may even amaze us. Perhaps Jesus is still among us, present in others, but we fail to recognize him.

Msgr. Stephen J. Rossetti

CAUGHT IN A TRAP

**Broken was the snare,
and we were freed.** Psalm 124:7

I generally try not to hold grudges. But I did nurse one for many years. I had a falling out with someone very close to me. We worked together, we socialized, we made each other laugh. I still remember what caused the rift. It broke my heart. Although we traveled in the same circles, I rarely saw this person anymore. If our paths did cross, the room suddenly got cooler.

Years passed, and I learned that her daughter died suddenly and tragically. I went to the funeral. As I approached, she said, "I need a friend now more than ever." We hugged. It was as if I was released from a trap. I felt the anger and resentment drain out of me.

I wish I knew why I held on to it for so long. I can't think of one good thing it did for me except keep me apart from someone I cared for. I know of many families and friends separated by long-held grievances. Remaining in these self-styled traps is hardly ever worth it. Forgive and forget.

Dear God, free us from the snares that divide us.

Paul Pennick

Loving Us Into Loving

The cry of the Israelites has reached me. Exodus 3:9

Why, O Lord, don't you hear the cry of this suffering child I know whose anguish is palpable? How many laments does it take before you turn to us? The Israelites, slaves in Egypt, cried for 200 years before you beckoned to Moses from the burning bush.

Perhaps that bush had been burning all along, and Moses was the first to see and stop. At any rate, he paid a price for stopping to listen. You sent him to Pharaoh to free the people. We know the many trials Moses underwent in fulfilling this mission. No wonder, at the burning bush, he "hid his face...afraid to look at God."

Lord, you ask much of those you call. You ask everything. You call us to become blazing, inconsumable fires. You urge us to become prophets, liberators, healers. You teach us to feel others' suffering and to respond with mercy. The only way we can is if you come with us yourself and love us into loving.

Lord, in Christ you became one of us. Help us to become like you.

Mary Marrocco

LISTEN... AND HEAR

I am meek and humble of heart. Matthew 11:29

Prayer involves listening with the "ears of the heart." It is a listening that invites humility in order to be attuned to voices other than one's own and learn from them. Jesus asks that we learn from him, that we be meek and humble of heart. From the time we are very young, we first learn by listening. Words that deeply touch us we take to heart. We keep words of love and remember them.

We are asked by Jesus to be like him, and in prayer, as we listen to the loved stillness of our lives, the peace that kind of prayer brings becomes a part of us. We should rest a bit every day and take that time to hear what is good and gentle around us. The more we listen, the more humble we become—and the more we become what we are longing to hear.

Fr. James Stephen Behrens, O.C.S.O.

Recognizing Jesus in His Wounds

Blessed are those who have not seen and have believed.

John 20:29

"Seeing is believing," we sometimes say, but there are some things that must first be believed in order to be seen.

When the risen Jesus appears to his disciples and Thomas is finally present, what brings Thomas to his knees in astonishment, awe and that moment of "Aha!" is actually seeing for himself the wounds of Jesus. These wounds offer Thomas irrefutable proof that this is the same Jesus who suffered, died and is now risen.

We may think that Thomas had it easy; after all, he got to touch the wounds of Jesus. But our faith tells us that even though we can't physically see Jesus today, we can still recognize him as he continues to show us his wounds. When we encounter a homeless person, listen to a neighbor's account of job uncertainty, struggle to heal fractured relationships, try to relieve a loved one's physical pain or be present to their emotional anguish, we are encountering Jesus in his wounds among us. Jesus risen, here and now.

We believe, and we see.

Sr. Chris Koellhoffer, I.H.M.

March 27

UNFATHOMABLE LOVE

This man was innocent beyond doubt. Luke 23:47

As a child, I remember learning about Jesus' Palm Sunday journey through Jerusalem. Sister Pamela read to us the Bible stories with pictures of Jesus on the donkey, winding his way through the narrow streets, jubilant crowds hailing the new Messiah. She drew our attention to the sad expression on Jesus' face. In a very short time, she said, these same adoring people would be shouting for him to be crucified.

It was probably our first serious encounter with death and injustice. "Why, Sister? Why did Jesus have to die?" Gentle, patient Sister Pamela told us: "Because he loved us." I don't think we quite knew what to make of that, but if she said it, we knew it had to be true. Years later—especially as a parent—I began to understand Sister's words: An innocent man would shed his blood for our sins so that we could live forever. It is the story of the Lord's Passion, a story of love—a boundless, incomprehensible love.

Paul Pennick

LIKE A MOTHER LION

As the water flowed back, it covered the chariots and the charioteers of Pharaoh's whole army which had followed the Israelites into the sea. Not a single one of them escaped.

Exodus 14:28

This is one of the Bible's great stories of God's saving work. But it always produces a strange mixture of emotions in me: awe at the power of God, horror at its destructive use, confusion that the action of a good God could have such terrible results.

At the same time, this story always makes me chuckle at how scandalously jubilant the Israelites are when their enemies meet their horrific end!

To be sure, not every story in the Bible harmonizes with my preferred image of a gentle God. But violent as it is, this tale is still a love story. God's love for his chosen people is ferocious and one-sided. God is the mother lion, lashing out to protect her cubs, ready to tear limb from limb any creature that would harm them. How surprising to think that God could love with such intensity. How humbling to think that God could love me like that.

God, your love can be fierce. Do you love me like that?

Karla Manternach

Choosing God

They exchanged their glory
for the image of a grass-eating bullock. Psalm 106:20

I was speaking recently with an old friend who has left behind his faith and life within the Church. His words echoed these from the psalmist—he had left God for the "image" of a better life without the rules and obligations of religion. He felt called away from a life with our glorious God, just as once he had been called to it.

I suppose we all feel the tug once in a while to take up something new and different. We sometimes struggle with seeds of discontent that lie deep within us. But God gives us the marvelous gift of free will. We are free to choose to listen to the loud shouts and noise of the world and all its glitter. Or we can sit by the fire or kneel in a pew and hear the soft and gentle voice of our loving God calling us home. That's a choice between life and death, and I choose life.

God, help me to hear your voice in the midst of a noisy world.

Steve Givens

Little Miracles, Little Blessings

**The earth has yielded its fruits;
God, our God, has blessed us.** Psalm 67:7

My mother loved lilies of the valley. She had them in her wedding bouquet. When she and my dad bought their first house, she set aside a small shady space in our yard to grow these delicate little flowers. The soil in this area was rich and dark, and every spring when they bloomed, you could see how pleased she was with the new crop.

My job was to help water them and keep weeds out of the bed. It wasn't that difficult to take care of them, and, after a time, I grew to love the tiny bell-shaped blooms with their dark green leaves and subtle fragrance. Each year I marveled at how they would emerge so healthy and happy after a long and cold Midwestern winter. It remained a tender, lifelong connection between a mother and her son. Little miracles, I thought, little blessings from God.

Dear God, I am grateful for the beauty and bounty of the fruits of your earth.

Paul Pennick

TURNING IT OVER TO GOD

Have mercy on me, O God, in your goodness;
in the greatness of your compassion wipe out my offense.

Psalm 51:3

Standing in line for confession can be nerve-racking. Do we really have to talk about our love of gossiping or our seeming inability to parent without shouting? What will the priest think? And what does God think? How can we be forgiven?

This fearfulness sells God's mercy short. Consider the example of King David who, after having an affair and sending a friend to certain death, sits down to ask God's forgiveness in this most famous of the seven penitential psalms. David acknowledges his offense, but also is confident that God will cleanse his heart and renew his spirit.

Few of us commit sins as atrocious as David's. Yet, fearful of condemnation and damnation, we still hesitate to seek forgiveness. Let us remember this example and trust in God's compassion as we confess our errors, no matter how dark we believe our hearts to be.

Lord, I praise you for showing mercy when I repent of my offenses.

Melanie Rigney

What a Story!

Then beginning with Moses and all the prophets, he interpreted to them what referred to him in all the scriptures.

Luke 24:27

The disciples on the road to Emmaus—what a story! We can just imagine ourselves asking the anguished, utterly ironic question: "Are you the only visitor to Jerusalem who does not know of the things that have taken place there in these days?" Terrible things had taken place, ripping apart their hopes and their hearts.

It has always fascinated me that Jesus responded by showing them the Scriptures "beginning with Moses and all the prophets." I wonder what he said that had their hearts burning on the road. Along with the figure of the suffering Messiah, did he point out how God brought amazing life out of hopeless situations? The Red Sea parting, the whale unswallowing Jonah, the field of dry bones becoming living, breathing people?

Each time we are faced with some terrible thing, we need the stories of the Love that saves us, the Love that walks right beside us on the road.

Patricia Livingston

In-Your-Face Faith

O woman, great is your faith! Matthew 15:28

What faith did the woman have? Certainly, it can't have been very well developed. All that she knew about Jesus would have come from the reports she had heard from travelers passing through her town on their way north from Palestine. She can hardly have known much about Jesus. If she showed up in a parish today, the pastor would steer her into the RCIA program where she could get some instruction.

But what little faith the woman had, she put to use. She shouted at Jesus in the street to get his attention. She told him just what she wanted him to do for her. And she wouldn't take no for an answer. Hers was a real in-your-face faith. And that's what Jesus liked about it. He liked that face-to-face confrontation with her.

Undoubtedly, he'd like that kind of face-to-face confrontation with you and me, too.

Kevin Perrotta

God Dazzles Us Each Day

**Fear the Lord, you his holy ones,
for nought is lacking to those who fear him.** Psalm 34:10

"Fear of the Lord" is a misunderstood gift of the Holy Spirit. It doesn't mean we shake from alarm before God. Rather, it means we stand in wonder and awe before our God who is eager to dazzle us each day. How does God dazzle us? Truthfully, anything can be a door to divine bedazzling: the scent of pine, the hooting of an owl, the sweetness of a peach, the laughter of a child, the kindness of a stranger, the embrace of a friend, a line from Scripture, the brightness of the stars at night.

There is a paradox here: if we truly fear the Lord, we need not fear anything else. Why? Because our God is not only almighty, but also all-loving. In fact, God's almighty power is chiefly expressed as loving kindness and gentleness toward all.

Loving God, help me to be more open to all the ways you wish to dazzle me with your love today.

Sr. Melannie Svoboda, S.N.D.

'Radically' Free to Follow Christ

If you wish to be perfect, go, sell what you have and give to [the] poor... Matthew 19:21

Jesus has earlier explained that to be perfect means to love all without exception: enemies as well as friends, the unjust and the just. Here, Jesus declares that, in order to share what one has with those who have less, perfection also means a radical disinterest in accumulating stuff. This, he adds, is the way to "have treasure in heaven." This isn't the end, however. The final requirement is that we follow him. Radical disinterest in wealth and possessions is the way to be free enough to follow Christ.

The lesson to learn from Jesus' words is to cultivate the spiritual freedom to share what we have with those who have little. This in turn will free us enough to follow wherever the Lord may lead us. Could be risky, but the point of following Christ is to become anything and everything Christ leads us to be.

Mitch Finley

Pain Is a Wise Advisor

> Then he said to Thomas, "Put your finger here and see my hands, and bring your hand and put it into my side, and do not be unbelieving, but believe." Thomas answered and said to him, "My Lord and my God!" John 20:27-28

What makes Thomas a believer? Not seeing Jesus in divine splendor? Not hearing him preach a persuasive sermon? Not seeing him perform an incredible miracle? No; what makes Thomas a believer is simply touching the wounds of Jesus. Connecting with the suffering humanity of Jesus, his good friend, brings him to faith.

Isn't it the same for us at times? We, too, come to faith not through our strength, cleverness or achievements, but often through our pain and weakness. As someone has said, pain is a wise advisor. Often our pain brings us to our knees. Our wounds turn us into believers—especially if they are joined to the pain and wounds of Jesus, our good friend.

Wounded Jesus, may my pain and weakness lead me to greater faith and trust in you.

Sr. Melannie Svoboda, S.N.D.

A God Who Weeps

And Jesus wept. John 11:35

Jewish rabbis tell a story about the death of Moses. It's not in the Bible, but it has a beautiful message. Moses once said to God, "I have worked so hard and suffered so much for you and your people. Please don't let me die." But God replied, "You are human; you have to die." When the day came, God came down from heaven and took Moses in his arms. And when Moses died, God took his final breath with a kiss. And then, the rabbis say, a big tear rolled down the face of God.

In this gospel reading, Jesus is profoundly saddened over the death of his friend Lazarus. When he comes to the tomb, his emotions are deeply stirred. And then comes those wonderful words, the shortest verse in the Bible: "And Jesus wept." God weeping over the death of Moses is only a beautiful story; with Jesus, it really happened.

But that is not the end of the story. Death will not be the last word; death will not triumph. The last word is resurrection and eternal life sharing our pain.

Fr. Martin Pable, O.F.M. Cap.

The Lord Is With Us

> The angel of the LORD appeared to him and said, "The LORD is with you, O champion!" "My LORD," Gideon said to him, "if the LORD is with us, why has all this happened to us?"
>
> Judges 6:12-13

Listen up, all you champions out there! What's with this attitude of yours? Yes, God is with you! He's right here, right by your side, right within your soul! Of course he didn't cause these difficulties to happen, but he allows them for a reason beyond your comprehension right now. He wills for you only goodness and mercy all the days of your life. He's with you to help you bear your heavy load, to meet this challenge head-on. His name is Victory, his yoke is easy and his burden light. Why would he ever send you to walk the valley of darkness all alone? How could you ever hope to overcome if he were not Emmanuel, God-with-us?

Awake, rise from your sleep! Your time has come. You are not alone. You can do it; the Lord is with you.

Claire J. King

A Blunt Message

Woe to you, scribes and Pharisees, you hypocrites. You are like whitewashed tombs, which appear beautiful on the outside, but inside are full of dead men's bones and every kind of filth. Matthew 23:27

For some of us, Jesus too often shows his gentle and patient side with the Pharisees, far too willing to put up with their foolishness and testing of him. This is not one of those times. Jesus' message here is direct, blunt and not couched in a parable.

We all get fed up from time to time. This gospel passage reminds me of the movie *Network,* where the people throw open their windows and shout at the top of their lungs: "I'm mad as hell, and I'm not going to take it anymore!"

Certainly, we can't run around shouting at people every time we reach our limit. We have to restrain ourselves for civility's sake, peace in the family, calm in the workplace. But in the face of raging hypocrisy, terrible injustice, the strong preying on the weak, a fair dose of righteous anger is understandable. It may be exactly what Jesus expects.

Paul Pennick

Living in Christ

All of you are children of the light. 1 Thessalonians 5:5

The townsfolk of Capernaum are filled with awe and wonder as Jesus casts out the unclean demon. His words accomplish things! In the midst of all our problems, whatever they may be, this gives us hope: Jesus cares for each of us as if we were his very own self. God cannot do anything but love us.

Yet one of the hardest things for some people to believe is that they are loved by God. They so rarely meet people who think they are great and seek out their company. Little by little, they isolate themselves, feeling that they have to find their way through this life alone. This gospel reading shouts out the reality that this is not so! Jesus stands for us and with us, never against us.

If he ever seems to have forgotten you, remember that a simple complaint with a word of gratitude is permissible now and then.

Master, remember me, now, for I need you. I can't see you, and I'm afraid. Thank you for hearing me.

Sr. Kathryn James Hermes, F.S.P.

TODAY IS NOT THE END

**Because of his affliction
he shall see the light...** Isaiah 53:11

Whenever I hear the Passion read, it stirs up a great emotion. The crucifixion account is a gut-wrenching narrative. It is tempting to give into despair.

But in the back of my mind, I am sustained and given hope. I know that crucifixion is not the last word. This is not the end of the gospel. Our grief is intense, yes, but momentary. The resurrection is coming swiftly.

There are profound tragedies in all of our lives. Some are unspeakable losses; we are overwhelmed to the point of death.

But this is not the final word. In our own darkness, when we, too, feel abandoned, we are aware that this is not the end. The final chapter of Jesus' life and ours will be the same.

Msgr. Stephen J. Rossetti

TRUSTING IN GOD

Into your hands I commend my spirit. Psalm 31:6

These powerful words of the psalmist, made all the more sacred when Jesus uttered them on the cross, offer us profound freedom from the worries and cares that can overwhelm us. Of course, we have obligations and responsibilities that cannot be skirted merely by mouthing pious words, but having engaged our struggles and paid some price, we have to let go.

In the end, we give back to God all the work, sacrifice, joy and sorrow. At the end of the day, we do not belong to ourselves any more than we did at the beginning. These few words make a wonderful prayer at bedtime, or in the middle of the night if the cares of the day surface to tug at our hearts once again.

In the hands of God, our spirits find refreshment and renewal for what lies ahead. God knows best what we need and how best to ready us for what is coming. Though it takes some faith to pray these words from the heart, it is much harder to avoid them by putting all the burden on ourselves.

Lord Jesus, help me to pray these words in faith, trusting all things to your care.

Mark Neilsen

AN INCOMPREHENSIBLE LOVE

What God has made clean, you are not to call profane.

Acts 11:9

I can rush to judgment about certain things. The cashier in the grocery store is working too slowly, or my friend's late arrival indicates his irresponsibility. My inner critic can separate me from others, gradually leading to a toxic outlook on life.

If you have ever experienced this, this passage from Acts can remind us both that our source of frustration is something or someone God likely finds beautiful. Many people in the early Church felt that Gentiles could never be good Christians because they were not circumcised or did not follow Jewish law. Peter's vision makes it clear that this is not the case; God's love is deeper and fuller than we can comprehend, and any limits we place on it are artificial. When we find ourselves talking about "those people" or creating distance by being critical of everybody around us (including ourselves), remembering this truth could serve to open our hearts to the trove of God's infinite love.

David Nantais

MERCY AND PERFECTION

Be merciful, just as [also] your Father is merciful. Luke 6:36

This verse became a source of genuine freedom for me. When I was growing up, there was tremendous emphasis in spiritual training on "be perfect, just as your heavenly Father is perfect," the parallel passage to this verse in Luke (Matthew 5:48). There was great preoccupation with eliminating every imperfection and a constant focus on one's fault and guilt.

Then I heard a Scripture scholar say that he was convinced that a better capturing of what Jesus actually said was to be found in Luke's account of that same sermon. Weight was lifted off me in that moment. Perfection was impossible in the struggle of real living. I saw that it was precisely because I had not been perfect myself, because I had needed and received mercy from others, that I had begun to learn to be merciful. As the goal of spiritual life shifted, a new freedom opened in my heart.

Patricia Livingston

THE TOIL AND TEARS OF LIFE

Those that sow in tears
  shall reap rejoicing.
Although they go forth weeping,
  carrying the seed to be sown,
They shall come back rejoicing,
  carrying their sheaves. Psalm 126:5-6

How much practical wisdom is hidden in this simple agrarian image! And how starkly different the message is from the contemporary notion of one's right to go through life with ease and comfort!

The theme of Psalm 126 is gratitude, the unbounded joy at the Lord's "restoring the fortunes of Zion." Ultimately, what we are, have and enjoy comes from God. But the psalmist reminds us that our God-given life always follows something of a cycle—hard work before rest, struggle before success, pain before contentment, sorrow before joy. Life—all life, including the spiritual life—necessitates toil and tears, but promises a share of satisfaction. Sowing is tedious and taxing work, but the expectation of a future crop helps to make it bearable. A wise commentator noted that the worst notion we can plant in children is that they can expect to escape pain, struggle and hardship. What we ought to help them realize instead is that toil and tears are part of a normal life.

James E. Adams

The Beam in Our Eyes

Why do you notice the splinter in your brother's eye, but do not perceive the wooden beam in your own? Luke 6:41

A few years back, I heard stories of people moving out of pews in Catholic churches to avoid sitting next to a man or woman who was divorced. I never saw this happen, and I certainly hope it was rare when it did. Nowadays, divorce is unfortunately so commonplace that, if this kind of behavior were the norm, Sunday liturgies would see people in constant motion in search of a pew untouched by people from failed marriages.

This gospel passage is not about the pain of divorce. It's about hypocrisy and judging others. It's about having acute awareness of other people's failings while ignoring our own. Although we may not be among the seat-changers, we need to think about that beam in our eye and forget about the splinters we see elsewhere. And, remember, every pew is filled with sinners.

Paul Pennick

LISTENING FOR THE LORD

I have seen the Lord. John 20:18

We are all familiar with the phrase "seeing is believing." For Mary, something more was necessary. She sees the Risen Lord and mistakes him for someone else. She truly sees him only when he calls her by name. It is Jesus who initiates her ability to truly see and recognize him. And she does so with great joy.

Our world abounds with images of Jesus to remind us of the centrality of his place in life. Yet it would seem that there is something more involved in seeing Jesus as he is in this life. We pray to hear his voice through those whom he speaks—be it those in ecclesial authority, the voice of the poor or the voices of those who live and speak God's word to us. The more we pray, the more we shall be able to recognize the many ways in which the Lord calls to us here and now.

Fr. James Stephen Behrens, O.C.S.O.

GRATEFUL FOR WHAT WE HAVE

Serve the LORD with gladness. Psalm 100:2

Last winter was an especially brutal one with plenty of snow and bitterly cold temperatures. By early January, I was feeling a desperate need to escape to a warm climate for a few days. Circumstances, however, made that impossible.

When I knew I couldn't do anything to change the situation, I prayed instead for a deeper awareness of God's presence in the midst of the bleak weather. That Sunday, after yet another ice storm, I walked into church feeling exasperated and devoid of joy. As I knelt down, I was suddenly overwhelmed by the beauty of the dozens of brilliant red poinsettias that filled the sanctuary. In fact, I was so moved that tears came to my eyes. I realized later that the same sight in the midst of summer would probably have escaped my attention altogether. Maybe we don't need more of everything as much as we need a deeper appreciation for what is right in front of us.

Jesus, make me more grateful for what you have given me.

Terri Mifek

Touching the Risen Lord

They have taken the Lord from the tomb, and we don't know where they put him. John 20:2

In the various resurrection accounts, when the followers of Jesus discover the empty tomb, they experience shock, fear, agitation, questioning and even tears. Only after these same followers see, hear and touch the Risen Jesus do they experience amazement, joy, peace, gratitude and understanding. The contrast is significant. It reminds us that times of turmoil, pain, doubt and confusion may not mark the end of faith, but may be a necessary stage toward greater faith and understanding.

Where are you on any given Easter Sunday? Are you experiencing fear, tears or agitation? Or are you closer to peace, joy and understanding? Wherever you may be, the Risen Jesus is beside you, eager to share the power of his resurrection with you. It is a power that enables us to trust, to love, to forgive or even just to hang on. Let us reach out in prayer today to touch the sacred wounds of the Risen Lord!

Risen Jesus, give me the grace I need today to trust, to love, to forgive or even just to hang on.

Sr. Melannie Svoboda, S.N.D.

Very Good News!

They put him to death by hanging him on a tree. This man God raised [on] the third day... Acts 10:39-40

Recall your lowest moments. What made them so terrible? Loss? Humiliation? Death? Suffering? Torment? I can remember my lowest points and what I needed to hear. It was simple: good news. I yearned for good news. Good news, not just for me, but for those I loved who suffered, who died, who were buried.

Well, here it is. Here's the best news of all: We're not alone in our suffering. God is there with us, in the thick of it, torn and buried. But now the tomb is empty. He is raised, and so are we, and so are all those who live and die in Christ. To be loved like this by the God who created us, to be embraced and lifted like this for eternity? Such very, very good news.

Alleluia, Jesus is Lord!

Amy Welborn

YOU ... FOOD ... LOVE

While they were still incredulous for joy and were amazed, [Jesus] asked them, "Have you anything here to eat?" They gave him a piece of baked fish; he took it and ate it in front of them. Luke 24:41-43

Old habits die hard—habits like a mother's desire to care for a child. So even though, after a long day at school and theater rehearsal, my seventeen-year-old daughter could throw her own dinner together while I took care of other things, I find myself insisting on getting her food.

There's no nobility on my part. There's just a primeval satisfaction involved in setting down a plate of food in front of your tired, hungry and frustrated child. There is not much you can do for her. But you can do this. Your presence, plus food, equals love.

Jesus, risen from the dead, spoke to his amazed disciples. He showed them his wounds. And then, in utter, everyday simplicity, he asked them for something to eat. His presence, plus food, equals love.

Risen Lord, I rejoice in your love.

Amy Welborn

'OFFERING IT UP'

...in my flesh I am filling up what is lacking in the afflictions of Christ on behalf of his body. Colossians 1:24

This statement of Paul's was utterly puzzling to me for many years. What could it mean that something was lacking in the afflictions of Christ? But in the last few years, this concept helped me greatly to find some meaning in the terrible sufferings of my sister who recently died. After her diagnosis, she said to me, "When we were growing up, the nuns taught us to 'Offer it up.' I am offering it up, but why does God want it? What is God going to do with it?"

Pope John Paul II wrote in his encyclical *On the Christian Meaning of Human Suffering* that in the mystery of the Body of Christ, a suffering person in any part of the world and in any time in history shares in the work of redemption. We serve the salvation of our brothers and sisters.

It matters greatly to me to know that my sister was part of the transformation of us all.

Patricia Livingston

Questions Lead to Wisdom

But they did not understand the saying, and they were afraid to question him. Mark 9:32

It is easy to understand why the disciples were reluctant to question Jesus' strange teachings about being killed and then raised from the dead. Are you ever afraid to question God? Are you fearful of questioning others? Questions are tools for wisdom and learning. They are an admission that we are willing to admit we don't always have the answers. Questions are good companions for the spiritual journey.

When you find yourself fearful of questioning, turn and learn from the child within you. Jesus brought a child before the disciples. He put his arms around that child, insisting that we must all become like children. He identified with the child. As I picture the scene of Jesus and the child, it occurs to me that children are generally not afraid to ask questions. They are naturally inquisitive and eager to learn.

Jesus, the child in me wants to ask you a question: Do you who are mighty know what it is to be small?

Sr. Macrina Wiederkehr, O.S.B.

'FOLLOW ME'

As Jesus passed on from there, he saw a man named Matthew sitting at the customs post. He said to him, "Follow me."

Matthew 9:9

In Rome, you can see the famed Caravaggio painting of this moment in the back corner of a smaller church in the center of the city. Out of the deep shadows steps Jesus. His outstretched hand points in the direction of a group of men at a table, and one of those men extends his own hand, gesturing back toward himself.

Me?

In Rome, you also see this: churches built over the tombs of young, innocent martyrs, magnificent churches built by churchmen and noblemen anxious to compensate for their sins, set snugly along cobblestone streets trod by pilgrims rich and poor, saints and sinners and all in between. All of us, some for better reasons than others, responding out of our own weakness, to the call.

Me? Jesus, yes. I will follow you.

Amy Welborn

All the Power We Need

He summoned the Twelve and gave them power... Luke 9:1

The very first fragment of this gospel sentence took my breath away, and so I stopped for reflection before finishing the sentence. I want to own it, as I put myself in the company of the Twelve. These words are meant for all. We have been summoned by Christ. We, too, are anointed ones who have been given power.

Let this be the heart of your prayer today. You have been summoned and given power. The power you are given is Christ Power. That is why Jesus explains to the disciples that when they go forth to heal and teach, it is unnecessary to take a lot of stuff along. "Take nothing on your journey," Jesus says. The power he has bequeathed to them is quite enough. Perhaps we, too, can practice believing that.

Jesus, you are my power and my grace. You are my walking staff. Your power is enough for me.

Sr. Macrina Wiederkehr, O.S.B.

PRAISE GOD!

Lord, teach us to pray just as John taught his disciples.

Luke 11:1

Jesus' answer to his apostles' request never fails to interest and challenge me. For he offers more than a prayer whose words are to be repeated. He offers a pattern—a model that involves praising and acknowledging God before we say another word.

Well, in reflecting on my own prayer life, I have to be honest and admit that honoring and praising God for being God is not always the first thing on my mind. Usually someone else comes first—namely, me. My desires, my aggravations, my questions, my pain.

St. Paul says that we do not know how to pray as we ought—meaning, in part, we don't know what to pray for. In putting praise of God first in my heart and in my words instead of my own ego, I take a first step in learning.

Lord, teach me to pray.

Amy Welborn

A Wellspring of Hope

Then they went away quickly from the tomb, fearful yet over-joyed... Matthew 28:8

"Fearful, yet overjoyed." How could the fear of these women possibly be described? How could the joy? The utter horror of Jesus' arrest and crucifixion is now followed by an earthquake, an angelic appearance and the tomb of Jesus empty!

Reeling from the unimaginable reversals, they hurry to announce the news to the disciples. I think it is amazing that they could even move. Then they come upon Jesus himself. It says, they "embraced his feet." I think their knees just gave out from the intense tremors of the earthquake in their own hearts. He was dead, tortured, broken. Now he's here on the road—greeting them—alive again!

The Easter story is the wellspring of our most unimaginable hope, hope in God's power to bring life out of death. Hope that all our fears can be brought to joy. Jesus tells us: "Do not be afraid," not only for our physical death, but for all the other endings, devastations and breakings.

Patricia Livingston

Singing a New Song

Sing to the Lord a new song... Psalm 98:1

Perhaps we're counted among them at this moment, the many in our world struggling to sing a new song. In that choir is the person longing to overcome addictive behavior; the mother caught in an abusive relationship that threatens her life and the safety of her children; the widow, widower, orphan who can do nothing but weep over the loss of a loved one; the immigrant or refugee displaced from all that sings of home and the familiar.

When our pain is so profound that the words catch in our throat, when terror, despair, numbness cause us to lose the melody, our faith assures us that even then, God continues to sing in us. What is the new song that God is calling us to enter into today?

Sr. Chris Koellhoffer, I.H.M.

Reflecting God's Goodness

But there will be glory, honor, and peace for everyone who does good, Jew first and then Greek. Romans 2:10

When I read these words, I immediately thought of my parents. Because of their goodness to me, and to so many others, I have always felt a spontaneous joy in honoring them. And I hope to continue honoring them when we are reunited in heaven. That will be one of heaven's great joys.

We can feel a desire to honor all good people whom we have come to know. Good people can be found in all cultures, for all people have the gift to reflect the goodness of the One who made them. One of the joys of life is to be gratefully aware of this goodness, wherever we may discover it.

Lord, keep my eyes open to the goodness in others, and to the goodness that exists in this world.

Fr. Kenneth E. Grabner, C.S.C.

A Humble Person's Prayer

Give me neither poverty nor riches;
[provide me only with the food I need;]
Lest, being full, I deny you,
saying, "Who is the Lord?"
Or, being in want, I steal,
and profane the name of my God. Proverbs 30:8-9

I know it's foolish to think that the quality of prayer may depend on articulating precisely the right things—as if the more cleverly worded prayers somehow had a better chance of attracting God's attention than prayers that are badly muddled.

Yet it surely can't hurt anything when our prayer is formulated with grace and precision, when our words help clarify and reveal rather than obscure what we are asking for. This passage from Proverbs strikes me as a profoundly wise prayer—and reminiscent of that "daily bread" petition in the Our Father. It is saying something like this: "Lord, I know my weaknesses. I realize that I probably can't handle either poverty or wealth very well. So give me what I need to live day by day. If I have too much to consume, I'm afraid I'll get sated and forget all about you and my spiritual duties." This is a humble prayer, the plea of somebody who is content to live modestly rather than to try doing great things.

James E. Adams

April 30

Forgiven on Every Side

Happy is he whose fault is taken away, whose sin is covered. Psalm 32:1

A number of years ago, I was coordinating the RCIA program in our parish and was preparing candidates to receive the Sacrament of Reconciliation for the first time. One of them, a middle-aged man, had more than the usual "jitters" about approaching the sacrament. He hinted at the terrible things he had done in years past and wondered aloud how God could ever forgive a person like him.

When the date to receive the sacrament arrived, he paced nervously back and forth awaiting his turn. What a relief, then, to see his beaming face when he reentered the body of the church. He shared with us later that, as he poured his heart out in Confession, he felt completely embraced by a loving God. That experience also made possible a breakthrough: Knowing himself so welcomed by God opened this man's heart to love and to forgive himself as well.

Loving God, help me to see my life through your compassionate eyes.

Sr. Chris Koellhoffer, I.H.M.

Asking the Right Question

> He said to him the third time, "Simon, son of John, do you love me?" Peter was distressed that he had said to him a third time, "Do you love me?" and he said to him, "Lord, you know everything; you know that I love you." [Jesus] said to him, "Feed my sheep." John 21:17

You can take all kinds of tests and inventories that will help you decide how to spend your time, resources and money. Personality types, charisms, gifts, talents. You can figure it all out with the right assessment, if you want.

All of that might be helpful at one time or another. But if we're not careful, we might be looking for the answer to the wrong question. If you're like me, that question is usually a variation of, "What's going to make me happy?" Perhaps that's the wrong question. Perhaps the question we should be answering isn't even our question at all.

"Do you love me?" Lord, I love you. What do you want me to do?

Amy Welborn

Rooted in Reality

Our help is in the name of the Lord,
who made heaven and earth. Psalm 124:8

When the computer makes a strange noise and the screen goes dark, I may be profoundly distressed, but I know where to go for help. The same is true if a little light flashes on the dashboard, the newspaper fails to arrive on time or part of the roof blows off in a storm. Such problems can be fixed. Help can be had.

But what if the doctor tells me an unusual spot has appeared on the x-ray of my lung? Or I discover I have been betrayed by a dear and trusted friend? Or that my child has been injured in a terrible car accident? If such things were to happen, where's the help?

Faith in God is often caricatured as an escape from reality, a fantasy of wishful thinking. But in my most trying moments, I have been able to immerse myself in reality only by finding help in God and in those who came in God's name.

In the hope that the conviction of this psalm verse will be with me when I need it most, I like to repeat it to myself from time to time. That way, I can be rooted in the reality of heaven and earth.

Mark Neilsen

FINDING JESUS OUTSIDE OF CHURCH

And all day long, both at the temple and in their homes, they did not stop teaching and proclaiming the Messiah, Jesus.

Acts 5:42

The disciples proclaimed Jesus as the Messiah at the temple (we would expect that) and in their homes (we might not expect that). The truth is, it is often easier to practice our faith inside a church than outside a church. Has anyone ever cut you off in the church parking lot right after Mass? If so, were you tempted to respond in a decidedly non-Christian way?

A question to reflect on today is this: How do I proclaim Jesus in places outside of church—in my home, at work, in the grocery store, on the freeway, in a doctor's office, in a restaurant, in the park, on a bus, at a sporting event? Do I interact in a kind and respectful way with individuals often overlooked or taken for granted: a store clerk, the guy who changes my oil, a letter carrier, a waiter or waitress, a maintenance man, a cleaning lady?

Jesus, help me to proclaim your name through my kindness and respect toward everyone I meet today.

Sr. Melannie Svoboda, S.N.D.

Praise God for Second Chances

He said to him in reply, "Sir, leave it for this year also, and I shall cultivate the ground around it and fertilize it; it may bear fruit in the future. If not you can cut it down." Luke 13:8-9

This conversation between the landowner and the gardener makes me want to weep. I could have been that tree, chopped down without hesitation. God could have let me be defined by my times of departure or periods of lukewarm faith. After all, I wasn't doing much for his field other than taking up sun, water and space, and bearing no fruit.

But in his kindness, he granted me the respite of time, the merciful gift of a second chance. He was the patient gardener who tended to my roots and pruned my branches and waited for me. In the fertile ground of humility, I took nourishment and my clipped branches began to blossom. Now I am a tree that bears fruit.

Let's praise God for second chances. Let's be slow to judge the value or condition of other trees.

Kristin Armstrong

AN INVESTMENT
IN HUMANITY

… **keep in mind the words of the Lord Jesus who himself said, "It is more blessed to give than to receive."** Acts 20:35

Every week I receive at least a dozen mail requests for donations. I believe in assisting others, but the volume is overwhelming. Yet the photo of a hungry, raggedly clothed child is difficult to ignore. True, some requests may not be genuine, but we are expected to help one another.

It would be a wonderful commentary on human nature if prosperity would lead one to generosity, but that often is not the case. The sick, hungry and homeless all cry out for assistance in our day as in the days when Jesus walked the earth. A gift of money, material or physical work produces two blessings: one to the person who receives it and one to the person who gives it.

When we give, we feel uplifted, knowing we are doing something good. We are investing in humanity and supporting a cause much bigger than ourselves.

Fr. James McKarns

Life's In-Between Moments

Glorify the Lord... Psalm 147:12

A woman in Los Angeles found a lost and negotiable check worth hundreds of thousands of dollars. She returned it to its owner, who rewarded her for returning the check. The woman gratefully accepted the money, saying she would put it aside for a "rainy day."

While there was no mention of God in the newspaper account, there was mention about how there are some real good people in this world. Indeed, the works of the Lord are great. We may look to the beauty of the sky or the smile of a baby to measure his greatness. But it is important to remember that he is at his best in life's in-between moments—those moments sandwiched between the glorious heights, when we do our best to return what was thought lost. It could be a check lying at our feet, an apology to one we may have hurt or a simple letter of thanks for a kindness received and long taken for granted.

Fr. James Stephen Behrens, O.C.S.O.

HE IS WITH US ALWAYS

But now, compelled by the Spirit, I am going to Jerusalem.
What will happen to me there I do not know... Acts 20:22

It seems I have spent much of my life surrounded by young people looking anxiously toward the future: students, my children, their friends. Currently, it is my daughter, who is researching colleges intently, determined to find the "perfect" place and convinced that if she makes the wrong choice, her life will be thrown off course. Maybe forever!

What she doesn't understand, but will eventually, is that while it's true that some situations are better than others for us, God is with us in all of them. We do our part to discern and decide—"compelled by the Spirit," as Paul was—but the truth is, just like Paul, we just don't know what will happen to us when we arrive. And also like Paul, in all of those places, we find peace, not in where we are, but in who's with us—always.

Lord, I don't know what the future holds, but I'm joyful that you'll be with me there.

Amy Welborn

Openness and Humility

On a sabbath he went to dine at the home of one of the leading Pharisees... Luke 14:1

Although often in open conflict with many of the Pharisees, Jesus apparently did not hesitate to accept an invitation to dine with them. How different his attitude is from mine. I find it easier and much more comfortable to simply avoid the people whose views conflict with mine and the situations where my integrity will be questioned or where I risk outright rejection. Going into a room filled with people who were openly hostile was a sign of the kind of interior freedom Jesus had that few of us experience.

Jesus always backed up his words with actions. On this occasion, he not only spoke of the importance of humility, he underscored his willingness to stay engaged with those who were not yet open to him. While he didn't shirk from speaking up, he also did not simply avoid those who opposed him.

Lord, keep my heart open as I encounter people and situations I find threatening.

Terri Mifek

Secure in the Arms of God

Like a weaned child on its mother's lap,
[so is my soul within me.] Psalm 131:2

As a child, I remember contemplating the exact location of my soul. I wondered where this spirit resided, this inner life that only God could see. Did it live in the pit of my stomach, in the beat of my heart or in my growing and ever-inquisitive mind?

I now no longer care about the "where" of my soul, but I am as sure as ever that my soul exists and more clearly defines who I am than any other aspect of my being. As I get older, I find myself more and more secure in the relationship between my soul and my God, for I feel increasingly like this weaned child, satisfied and secure but still growing, safe in the arms of God, the source of my sustenance and life.

God, nurture and hold my soul close.

Steve Givens

Loving God Despite the Suffering

Paul and Silas were praying and singing hymns to God as the prisoners listened... Acts 16:25

Paul is the poster child for suffering. He endured much for his faith—as he himself took pains to report. In this passage alone, we see Paul stripped, beaten, imprisoned and bound to a stake. And what is he doing in the midst of it all? He is praying! He is singing! Even the earthquake that opens his cell is less surprising than his tranquility in the face of his own hardship.

There was a time in my life when I believed I had to go looking for suffering in order to be closer to Jesus. I thought that pain would teach me about the cross, so I sought it out. Now I understand that we all suffer. The challenge is to accept the suffering that inevitably comes to us with as much grace as we can. Like Paul, who makes no attempt to escape from hardship even when the opportunity arises, I think our task is to be a good sport about our suffering and to remain grateful to God in spite of it.

Lord God, my life is sometimes hard, but all that I have is from you. Thank you.

Karla Manternach

Wisdom Prevails

Compared to light, [Wisdom] takes precedence;
  for that, indeed, night supplants,
  but wickedness prevails not over Wisdom. Wisdom 7:29-30

So often Scripture assures us that wickedness will not prevail, that goodness is stronger than evil and love more powerful than hate. Yet my default position seems to be the exact opposite, at least in the short run: It looks like a lot of good people get crushed by powerful forces that look just plain evil.

This passage from Wisdom suggests that my looking may be part of the problem. Looking depends upon light in the physical realm, and darkness can overcome that. In the physical world of sight and sense, yes, evils like war, addiction, murder and various forms of mayhem may prevail, just as darkness overcomes light. But there is more to life than physics.

Jesus, the living Wisdom of God, reveals a life that goes beyond the physical. Destroyed by jealousy and hate, crushed by the power of Rome, Jesus was killed, but not extinguished.

Risen Lord, strengthen my faith in what I cannot see yet long to believe.

Mark Neilsen

Forgiving as Jesus Would

[Stephen] fell to his knees and cried out in a loud voice,
"Lord, do not hold this sin against them." Acts 7:60

Stephen demonstrates an extraordinary largeness of heart as he's being stoned to death. In his words, we hear echoes of Jesus' dying plea: "Father, forgive them, for they know not what they're doing."

So often we hear people who have been wronged remark that they can forgive, but they can never forget the hurt. Yet Stephen begs God to have a lapse of memory, to not even remember what's been done against him.

This amazing embrace of absolute forgiveness is so counter-cultural. Several years ago, after the brutal murder of five Amish schoolchildren in Nickel Mines, PA, the Amish community also did the unthinkable. As they grieved the tragic loss of their precious little ones, they reached out to the wife of the murderer, attended his burial and supported a fund for his family.

Loving God, give me the largeness of heart to forgive as you do.

Sr. Chris Koellhoffer, I.H.M.

When We Haven't Got a Prayer

> In the same way, the Spirit too comes to the aid of our weakness; for we do not know how to pray as we ought, but the Spirit itself intercedes with inexpressible groanings.
>
> Romans 8:26

When all is going well, when we seem to be on top of the world, when God's power seems to be flowing directly into our lives, how easy it is for us to see and feel the presence of the Spirit! How easy it is to pray! But what about when nothing seems to be going well, when we've sunk to the bottom, when God seems to be a million miles away? All we seem able to do is groan and moan and pickle in our exasperation.

Do not despair, do not even lament that you are in this situation, but be hopeful because the Spirit is probably flying to your aid; such is the suggestion of St. Paul. It's natural to assume in such situations that the Spirit is gone, but it's not true, St. Paul is saying. The Spirit is present in our weakness. The Spirit turns weakness on its head. Our groaning, pain and exasperation do not mean that all is lost. In fact, our moans and groans may well be on their way to becoming our prayer, thanks to the Spirit.

Holy Spirit, may I never forget that you can—and want to—turn my suffering into prayer.

James E. Adams

May 14

Praise God as Sacrifice

Offer to God praise as your sacrifice... Psalm 50:14

On first glance, this might seem too easy. Even a bit of a cop-out. How could praise be the equivalent of a concrete sacrifice? Compared to the first of your flock or harvest, your money or your time, it doesn't seem as if saying words of praise to God could require anything of me.

Ah, but maybe it does. When things are not going well. When life hasn't turned out as I planned or hoped. When I'm experiencing loss or disappointment. Then, yes, perhaps putting aside my own desires, plans and conception of what life should be like does, indeed, require a sacrifice—a far greater sacrifice than anything concrete or material, in fact. As St. Ignatius wrote in his prayer, "Take Lord, receive all my liberty," it might be the greatest sacrifice I can make today.

Lord, I praise you for everything in my life, past and present.

Amy Welborn

The Best Is Yet to Come

He will wipe every tear from their eyes, and there shall be no more death or mourning, wailing or pain, [for] the old order has passed away. Revelation 21:4

The promise of new life echoes repeatedly throughout the entire Easter season. This promise is God's greatest gift, but it is not meant to take away our appreciation for this life. Our present life is also a gift. God wants us to be thankful for it, to enjoy it and to share our blessings. But we know this life is incomplete. We long for something more.

Many years ago, at the end of an Easter homily, I said, "You know, I can't wait for this new life to come." And today, I am even more excited by it. For if God promises the fullness of life in the resurrection, I will be more alive then than I am now. I will be more aware of God's love and more conscious of his beauty shining through all of his creation.

This life is good, Lord, but help me to believe that the best is yet to come.

Fr. Kenneth Grabner

Surrender to the Birthing

Peace I leave with you; my peace I give to you... Do not let your hearts be troubled or afraid. John 14:27

What gives us peace? What keeps our hearts from being troubled or afraid?

One answer that touches me I heard from a lovely older woman named Betty. It was in a summer program class I was teaching at Notre Dame, and we were talking about dealing with troubles in life: difficulties, challenges, losses. Betty shared with us a process that really helped her. She said, "Someone once taught me this secret: When we are sad, in pain, very worried about something, ask: 'Could this be labor?' And then, instead of fighting the pain or sadness or fear, give in to it, letting it take you to the birthing. Surrendering to the birthing brings with it hope, a trust that some new life is coming to your soul, is coming to the world."

Mothering God, source of life for all of us, help us trust that when we are troubled and afraid, you are with us, helping us give birth to life.

Patricia Livingston

GOD IS ALWAYS NEAR

When you see these things happening, know that the kingdom of God is near. Luke 21:31

In this passage, Jesus warns his disciples of the hardship and adversity that is to come. In the Bible, it is common to talk about suffering as a sign that the kingdom of God is near. Especially in the Gospel of Luke, this means that the end times are coming.

These days, we aren't apt to start checking our watches for the end of the world every time we experience pain. But even we can understand suffering as a sign of the nearness of God. There is no surer sign that God is with us than when we are in pain. During the dark times of our lives, the very times when we might question whether God cares for us, God is at hand. God is like the neighbor who brings a covered dish and checks to see if there is anything else she can do to help, anything at all. God will not forget the ones he loves.

Loving God, help me to know that you are always near.

Karla Manternach

BOWING TO GOD'S WILL

If you remain in me and my words remain in you, ask for whatever you want and it will be done for you. John 15:7

We tend to think, "I should be able to ask for anything and get what I ask for, especially if what I ask for is good—the cure of someone with an incurable disease, the rescue of a marriage, peace instead of war . . ." and so forth.

Of course, we know this doesn't happen. We've tried that kind of prayer, and we didn't get what we prayed for. So what's the deal here? Go back to the first part of the sentence: "If you remain in me and my words remain in you..." Maybe the true meaning is something like this: If we perfectly remain in the Risen Christ, and his words remain perfectly in us, then we will ask only for what God in his wisdom will give.

But we never do these things perfectly, do we? We can't use these words of Jesus as if they are a magic formula. All prayers should end with a bow of obedience to the ultimately mysterious will of God.

Lord Jesus, remain in me and let your words remain in me.

Mitch Finley

Why Do We Have the Needy?

For he shall rescue the poor man when he cries out,
and the afflicted when he has no one to help him.
He shall have pity for the lowly and the poor;
the lives of the poor he shall save. Psalm 72:12-13

I happen to live in a city where there are hundreds of nonprofit organizations, not to mention charitable and civic service groups plus thousands of student volunteers. There are almost a dozen food pantries, four homeless shelters, government human service agencies, a free medical clinic, workforce development and vocational rehab, counselors, mediators, elder care coalitions and recovery programs. There is also a seemingly never-ending stream of hungry people, homeless people, people out of work and people in need.

I often wonder how this can be. With all of this generosity, why does the need still persist? "This is what the poor are for," Peter Maurin, cofounder of the Catholic Worker, once wrote, "to give to the rich the occasion to do good for Christ's sake."

I am not sure Maurin's Easy Essay is the final answer to this oft-asked question, but it is one I need to ponder.

Claire J. King

Enduring It All

In the world you will have trouble, but take courage, I have conquered the world. John 16:33

Jesus seems to be preparing his disciples for the struggle and adversity they will face when he is no longer with them. We know well what his followers would encounter. We are all too familiar with the horrors of this world. Every news report reminds us of the cruelties that human beings inflict on one another, individually and on a large scale. In the face of such ugliness, it sometimes defies belief that the Spirit is always and everywhere present.

But if the crucifixion tells us anything, it is that Jesus knew first-hand all that human beings are capable of. He himself experienced the full intensity of our hatred and brutality. Christ endured it all. In a real way, he does endure it whenever somebody suffers. Yet in spite of everything, Christ claimed us for himself. He claimed the whole world, just as it is.

Jesus, you want this world for yourself, flawed as it is. Help me to grasp hold of you as you have grasped hold of me.

Karla Manternach

In Communion, I Know Him

If you know me, then you will also know my Father. From now on you do know him and have seen him. John 14:7

This is so true for me: Jesus is where my faith begins and ends, the Alpha and Omega, just as Revelation describes him. For the universe and its mysteries are so deep, and the Creator of it all is so...beyond me. If you've ever read St. Augustine's *Confessions*, you know that the first few paragraphs of this great work by one of the greatest, most brilliant theologians are composed almost completely of questions addressed to God—questions that are never really answered because they can't be, not in this life, not by us. There are many reasons I resonate with the *Confessions*, beginning with all those questions, and Augustine's honesty in posing them. How can I know? It can all threaten to implode in my brain, these deep questions.

But Jesus? Loving, merciful to the point of the Cross, and rising from the dead? Speaking and living out mercy? Thanks to that gracious mercy, I'm brought into communion, and I know.

Amy Welborn

THE GRACE TO BELIEVE

When he entered the house, the blind men approached him and Jesus said to them, "Do you believe that I can do this?" "Yes, Lord," they said to him. Matthew 9:28

I recently had a request for prayers from a young Christian friend. "Please pray that I believe in grace," he said. In the conversation that followed over a cup of coffee, he explained that for the first time in his young adulthood, he and his new wife were really struggling to respond as Jesus would as they witnessed the infidelity of one of their other young married friends. "I never would imagine that any of our friends would cheat on their spouse. How could they do this? It's against everything we've all believed in together."

"What is it that you have believed?" I asked. "That God is faithful," he replied. "And merciful and full of forgiveness. That's why I need grace," he explained. "The grace that our friends can accept these qualities of God and that he can show them these gifts through our words and actions."

Lord, I do believe that you can do this. Jesus, live your life out loud in mine.

Claire J. King

Loving as Jesus Loves

This is my commandment: love one another as I love you.

John 15:12

Jesus' standard of love is really high: his own example of loving. And what did that entail? First of all, Jesus' love was inclusive. He welcomed the poor and rich, Jew and Gentile, women and men, healthy and sick, young and old, timid and bold, charming and annoying. No one was outside his circle of loving—not even those who put him to death. And it was Jesus' love that enabled him to lay down his life for us. The laying down of our life for others can take many forms: a single sweeping gesture—like a firefighter entering a burning building—or the countless small acts of self-denial involved in sustaining a marriage, raising a child, living a religious commitment, serving in a particular ministry or enduring pain.

"Love one another as I love you." What a challenge that is! But the good news is this: Jesus, our friend, strengthens us in all our attempts to be inclusive and selfless in our loving.

Jesus, help me to enlarge the circle of my loving.

Sr. Melannie Svoboda, S.N.D.

Knowing How to Love

> Let your life be free from love of money but be content with what you have, for he has said, "I will never forsake you…"
>
> Hebrews 13:5

St. Augustine says we are made for love. But made for love does not mean we know how to love. Learning to love tells the story of our lives. As in any classroom, we often fail. In whatever absorbs us— work, meetings, sports, cooking, prayer—the call to love can be heard. We seek what we don't fully grasp, even when it is present. And in some ways, love is always present.

St. Paul dispels the myths. To love is not comfortable or easy. Not a surge of feeling, love is a great thirst. We are called into struggle to find rest. Paul tells us to open our lives to strangers and treat outsiders as angels in our midst. Prisoners must be shown care as if we were locked up together. Celebrate the promises made before God and the community. Do not fall under the spell of money. Because wealth is already present, our gifts can flow freely.

God, free us from the illusions of love.

Jeanne Schuler

When the Spirit Says "No"

> [Paul and Timothy]...had been prevented by the Holy Spirit from preaching the message in the province of Asia. When they came to Mysia, they tried to go on into Bithynia, but the Spirit of Jesus did not allow them... Acts 16:6-7

At first glance, these two divinely inspired "Nos" to Paul and Timothy seem startling. The two were traveling in Asia Minor with the goal of preaching the gospel. What could more clearly be the will of God than to preach the gospel at the next place on one's itinerary? Surely the answer would be "Yes." Instead, they were told "No" by the Holy Spirit. St. Luke, the writer of Acts, never says exactly how these messages from the Holy Spirit are given, but in other places, Luke notes that the Spirit uses prayer, visions, dreams—even throwing dice.

How they were told "No" to their plans isn't as important as the fact that it happened at all. Is there a message here for us? We need to be aware that the Holy Spirit can and does say "No" at times to our cherished plans—not just our neutral or selfish plans but even our plans to do good and noble things. But if the answer is "No" to one approach, we must do what Paul and Timothy did. Instead of going home in a huff, they remained open to the Holy Spirit and that very night got new directions.

James E. Adams

May 26

His Compassion Is With Us

> When he disembarked and saw the vast crowd, his heart was moved with pity for them, for they were like sheep without a shepherd; and he began to teach them many things.
>
> Mark 6:34

Jesus' heart is moved with pity for us too. When we remember how often he has helped us with problems too difficult to handle by ourselves, then we understand how his compassion has touched our lives. His compassion is our reason for hope. What Jesus has done in the past is a pledge of what he will do for us in the present.

I experience Jesus' compassion especially when I am confused. That happens occasionally when I am preparing a homily or writing an article. When no ideas come, I say to God, "This is for your people. What do you want them to hear?" And then, the ideas come! In his compassion, the Shepherd does not deprive his sheep of the guidance they need. His compassion is with us in our confusion, in our weakness and especially in our sinfulness.

Fr. Kenneth Grabner, C.S.C.

'It Was Very Good'

God looked at everything he had made, and he found it very good. Genesis 1:31

As the earth becomes home for things that fly and walk, creep and prowl, crawl and swim, the animal kingdom arrives with its vast array of personalities. Everything, both wild and tame, has its purpose. All that is created has a spark of the divine in it. Everything flows from the Infinite One; everything is proclaimed to be good.

It now appears that our loving creator wants someone on earth who is able to recognize and rejoice in all this goodness. There is a need for someone to love and care for the earth and its creatures and resources. The human person arrives on the scene. Each of us has been created with a hint of eternity in our being. In the divine image, we are created.

Take some time each day to help repair a part of creation that is suffering.

Sr. Macrina Wiederkehr, O.S.B.

Saving Grace

> When the afflicted man called out, the LORD heard,
> and from all his distress he saved him. Psalm 34:7

Considering this part of the Responsorial, we might be inclined to feel resentful and wonder, "Why did the Lord hear him and not me?" "He saved him from all of his distress? Really? I'd settle for just a little less distress in my life," we might say.

But thinking more about this assurance, we may realize that the Lord does save us from a great many distresses. In fact, we are assured that the Lord always hears our call; we just don't always recognize the saving—that close call on the highway, that lightning strike that occurred just a few feet away from us.

More important than physical saving, for many of us, is the need for spiritual rescuing.

Let's reflect today on the likelihood that our road to growing spiritually, and to being saved spiritually, may take us through some terrible trials. But we can handle those trials, assured that God goes with us and keeping in mind the end result—sharing eternal glory with him.

Terence Hegarty

When Will There Be Peace?

All these evils come from within and they defile. Mark 7:23

Our world continues to be plagued by violence, evil and hatred. Even after so many centuries of human "progress," humankind cannot rid itself of such evils. Where does it all come from?

Jesus tells us: "What comes out of a person, that is what defiles." And he gave us a frightening list: "evil thoughts, unchastity, theft, murder, adultery, greed, malice, deceit, licentiousness, envy, blasphemy, arrogance, folly" (verses 20-22). All of these evils in the world spring from their evil seeds in the human heart.

Our greatest contribution to goodness in the world is first to seek purity of our own hearts. We ask God to help rid our hearts of every evil impulse. We pray that, as the years pass and we continue to walk in God's way, our hearts will be slowly purified and filled with the divine goodness.

When each human heart across the globe has been thus purified, then there will be peace.

Msgr. Stephen J. Rossetti

Sharing God's Gift of Love

We love because he first loved us. 1 John 4:19

It is God's love that we return to him and that we share with each other. The love of God and our neighbor cannot be experienced as somehow separate. The way to one is through the other. I think it can be safely said that most of us assume love can come our way if and when we seek it with the proper charms. Today's media offer daily recipes of real love for those who feel they lack it. And yet the gift has been given and can only be experienced by giving it away.

Love is indeed a mystery in that the only way we can keep it is by losing it again and again. Such is the meaning of life and the discovery of God. The community of the Church is the place where we learn of the gifts bestowed on us by God and how best to share them.

Fr. James Stephen Behrens, O.C.S.O.

A Visit That Strengthens Us

After staying [in Antioch] some time, [Paul] left and traveled in orderly sequence through the Galatian country and Phrygia, bringing strength to all the disciples. Acts 18:23

Paul really kept on the move. This chapter alone tells of seven places he visited. We are told that as he traveled, he brought strength to all the disciples. We know from his letters that when he could not visit in person, he wrote to them.

When we visit or write or call, it can really make a difference. I recently had a weekend visit from someone who had not been here for a long time. We watched the sunset, tried out a recipe, cheered for a game, laughed at old stories, brainstormed new challenges and gave thanks for blessings. Saying good-bye, I felt how the visit had strengthened us. We need, as Paul and his disciples did, to have each other's company on this human journey.

Beloved God, in our visits and calls and letters, we are sharing more than ourselves—we are sharing you, who once traveled to where we are and strengthened us, showing us we are not alone.

Patricia Livingston

Asking Essential Questions

> He instructed them to take nothing for the journey but a walking stick—no food, no sack, no money in their belts. Mark 6:8

Imagine that someone you love is dying, and you want to see her one last time. Your sense of urgency is so strong that you focus only on getting to her as fast as possible. You have no time for anything else.

Jesus felt a similar sense of urgency in making sure that his message would be heard. The time was short, and people desperately needed to hear his words of love and hope. Jesus' focus was on spreading the message, not on concerns about food, a sack or a money belt.

Mark's Gospel invites me to ask an essential question about my life: Do I feel a sense of urgency to reflect on Jesus' message and allow it to bring the hope and joy God intends for me? Or am I often distracted by things that are less important?

Lord, may I open my heart to your words so that they may change my life.

Fr. Kenneth Grabner, C.S.C.

In God We Have Enough

Then, taking the seven loaves he gave thanks... Mark 8:6

We are often nagged by fear. We are worried that we will not have enough—enough time, energy, money, skill or whatever. We are aware of our very human limitations.

The disciples were likewise aware of their human limitations. They had but a few loaves and fish, and before them were 4000 hungry people. They did not have enough.

Jesus took what they had, blessed it, and, in God's overflowing generosity, fed the crowd with even more food left over. When we give what little we have to our infinite God, God makes it over flowing.

Today, as we begin our day, let us offer what we have to God, our few loaves and fish, and ask for the divine blessing. Then, in God, it will be enough.

Msgr. Stephen J. Rossetti

Following His Lead

He took the blind man by the hand and led him outside the village. Mark 8:23

Surely the blind man must have felt some apprehension when Jesus led him away from his familiar surroundings to be healed. I know there are few things I dislike more than feeling lost and unsure of where I am headed. When I recently encountered a bewildering detour on the way to visit a friend who had moved, I had to take a deep breath and pray not to panic. I eventually arrived safely, but the trip was not without some moments of confusion and distress.

At times our spiritual journey will deviate from the path we expected to follow. Maybe we have prayed for healing and things appear to be worse, or perhaps the rituals and prayer forms we have relied on have lost their appeal. We feel lost and aren't sure which way to turn, yet like the blind man, we sense that we must walk into the unknown, trusting that we will not be abandoned.

Faithful Guide, give me the courage to follow where you lead me.

Terri Mifek

Patron Saint of 'Good Grief'

Peter was distressed that Jesus had said to him a third time, "Do you love me?" and he said to him, "Lord, you know everything; you know that I love you." John 21:17

Peter provides much inspiration both to church leaders and to ordinary Christians because he learned so well the lesson of grievance deeply over his sins and failures—but then accepting forgiveness and moving on to respond with vigor to the next call of the Lord.

If we are caught up in denial, in remorse or in pseudo grief, we can easily be paralyzed and unfit to meet the next challenge in our spiritual journey. How often do we wallow in self-justification, self-doubt, self-recrimination, self-hatred—maybe even despair? But when we react as Peter did in heartfelt sorrow, when we look outward to God's mercy instead of inward to our own limited resources, we can accept ourselves in joyful humility. We can look again with more objective eyes on our gifts. We can begin to see the Holy Spirit working to strengthen our meager natural abilities—and working around our disabilities. We can realize again that God wants his sons and daughters—like Peter—to be on their feet in readiness, not on their bellies in discouragement.

St. Peter, help me to grieve deeply for my sins, and to seek and accept the forgiveness of God.

James E. Adams

Turning the Other Cheek

When someone strikes you on [your] right cheek, turn the other one to him as well. Matthew 5:39

A Scripture scholar's insight transformed this line for me. In first-century Palestine, left-handedness was seen as evil. People never used their left hands for any public task, even slapping a person. The only way to strike a person on the right cheek, using the right hand, is with a backhand. One could only strike "inferiors" backhanded: slaves, women and children. Striking an equal, a free man, with a backhand could incur legal punishment. Hence, Jesus' message: if someone treats you as an inferior by backhanding you on the right cheek, turn the other cheek to them and challenge them to treat you as an equal, a form of nonviolent resistance. It is an instruction about using inner strength in a noble way.

This call to respond with dignity is greatly needed in this time when verbal backhanding erupts in every forum. We need Jesus' call to stand up to contemptuousness not by striking back, but by fostering respect.

Patricia Livingston

Not This Story Again?

Lord, if you wish, you can make me clean. Luke 5:12

The story is so familiar. The point of the story has been driven home by countless preachers—and anyway, it is obvious: Sin is a kind of leprosy of the mind and heart; each of us has a deadly case; Jesus has come to heal us.

Can new light be shed on anything so well-known? Probably not. But is that the important question?

Each of us is painfully aware of at least some of our sins. Our feelings of failure, regret and shame are hard to bear. We may feel trapped in our sins, afraid that we cannot change even with divine help ("that may work for some people, but not for me"). We may not even be entirely sure we want to change, especially if change is going to require great effort.

The important questions, then, about the gospel story are those we ask about ourselves. After looking squarely at my sins and weaknesses, am I willing to come to Jesus and really ask him for healing? And when he answers, "I do will it; be made clean," will I listen to his words with faith in him?

Kevin Perrotta

Words of Encouragement

And a voice came from the heavens, saying, "This is my beloved Son, with whom I am well pleased." Matthew 3:17

Good coaches work their players hard, saying, "I know you can do better than that!" But good coaches also encourage their players with words such as these: "Good job!" "Way to go!" "I'm proud of you!" Today God encourages Jesus as he embarks on his public ministry.

Jesus comes to John to be baptized. At first John is reluctant to do this, for he realizes (to an extent) who Jesus is and feels unworthy. But Jesus urges him to baptize him. Immediately afterward, Jesus sees the "Spirit of God descending like a dove" and hears a voice saying those beautiful words quoted above.

It is heartening to know that Jesus himself needed encouragement from God during his lifetime. Sometimes that encouragement came directly—as it does here and later at the transfiguration. But often God's encouragement came indirectly to Jesus through his apostles, friends and those he served. Who encourages me in my life of faith? Whom do I encourage?

Sr. Melannie Svoboda, S.N.D.

An Awareness of God

Now this is eternal life, that they should know you, the only true God, and the one you sent, Jesus Christ. John 17:3

These joyful words tell us much about the meaning of our life. Our eternal life will be a dynamic loving relationship with God that will never be taken away from us. And the good news is that this relationship starts now. In this very moment, we can know that we are precious to God, and right now we can give thanks to God who penetrates every part of our lives. This is an essential point of the gospel message for me.

I can miss his presence, though, if I don't take time to be aware of it. The awareness grows in silent prayer and in the realization of God's guidance in my daily life. I believe this is a basic experience open to all of us. It is God's gift. All we have to do is take time for it. God will do the rest.

Lord, you are always within me, and everywhere around me. May I care enough today to notice you.

Fr. Kenneth Grabner, C.S.C.

THE SAFEST PLACE OF ALL

**The salvation of the just is from the LORD;
he is their refuge in time of distress.** Psalm 37:39

I've prayed many times for God to save me. I've asked God to make a lost wallet reappear. I've asked God to bring someone back from the dead. These requests aren't even in the same universe as each other, but that didn't occur to me at the time. Asking for God to do something is often, I think, a reflex. It is a reaching out to God and an acknowledgment of our own helplessness.

What does it mean for God to rescue us? For the record, I witnessed no resurrection, but I found my wallet where I left it. Did God let me down? As far as I know, God has not prevented painful things from happening to me. God has not taken away my suffering. But I believe God helps us in much the same way as the people in our lives who love us—by being there, by loving us while we are in pain. This doesn't remove the source of our suffering, but it is a kind of shelter. Love is a safe place in the storm. God is the safest place of all.

Karla Manternach

Loved by God

I pray not only for these, but also for those who will believe in me through their word... John 17:20

We're the ones Jesus was praying for in this long soliloquy after the Last Supper. He prayed for us to be in him and God so that "the world may believe that you sent me... and that you loved them even as you loved me" (John 17:21, 23).

Of all the things he could have prayed for on our behalf (charity, forgiveness, peace, generosity), he prayed that the peoples of the world would believe that God loves them. It strikes me that maybe I should adopt this as my only prayer. For one who deeply believes God loves him or her, all other suffering is eased.

Knowing we're loved by God releases us from the deep anxiety I believe we all carry that we're not truly loved, that we don't truly matter. That anxiety, I believe, drives people to shoot up a school, become a suicide bomber or erupt in road rage.

So let us pray, fervently, with Jesus that all will come to know they are loved by God.

Aileen O'Donoghue

Faith Transforms Fear

Daughter, your faith has saved you. Go in peace and be cured of your affliction. Mark 5:34

Her community deemed her an abomination. The days of bleeding stretched into years; she was impure and could not stand among the righteous. She could not fall to her knees like Jairus before Jesus and beg for help. A nameless outcast, she was not worthy to be heard. Hidden in the crowd, the bleeding woman reached out to touch his cloak—a silent plea for help.

Jesus searches for her. She is not yet healed. The bleeding stops, but she is much more than her affliction. "Your faith has saved you." We are tempted to forget where our greatness lies. We are not saved by magic; we do not disappear into failures and reemerge with success. Like the bleeding woman, our greatness lies in reaching out to those who love us in our brokenness. In fear, the beauty of our being slips from view. Faith transforms fear. From the depths of our smallness comes cause for celebration.

God, free me to reach out for you.

Jeanne Schuler

When Love Isn't Easy

> [Jesus said,] "But I say to you, love your enemies and pray for those who persecute you..." Matthew 5:44

Few teachings of Jesus in the gospels put us between a rock and a hard place like this one. No wiggle room here—at all. Do a little brainstorming on whom you might think of as your enemies. A dictionary defines "enemy" as: "someone who hates another; someone who attacks or tries to harm another; something that harms or threatens someone or something; a group of people (such as a nation) against whom another group is fighting a war."

Can you think of anyone that fits any of these categories for you? What about known terrorists like Osama bin Laden whom our government tracks down and kills? Jesus taught that we should love them too. Jesus taught us to love our enemies, even if those enemies have done some really, really horrible things to us.

Jesus, help me to love my enemies as you love them.

Mitch Finley

Sowing God's Word

Hear this! A sower went out to sow. Mark 4:3

I was raised on a 300-acre farm and have early memories of sowing the seeds of our crops—corn, oats, wheat, barley and hay. I especially recall Dad sowing alfalfa seed. When the ground was plowed and smoothed, he would walk through the fields carrying the seed and cranking our handheld sower. I would help by clearing rocks from the field.

I often wonder what images Jesus had in mind when he spoke of sowing seed. He said the seed is like the word of God and we are the soil. Frivolous distractions and excessive worldly cares are the thorns and weeds that choke the seed. Jesus assures us that if we are open and ready to receive his word, it will produce rich and lasting spiritual fruit in our lives.

Lord, we stand ready to receive your words of life.

Fr. James McKarns

THE FAITH TO SPEAK UP

Many rebuked him, telling him to be silent. But he kept calling out all the more... Mark 10:48

It can be tough to speak out when, all around, people are telling you to be quiet. Sometimes they say it directly, as here to Bartimaeus. Sometimes it's the loud silence of peer pressure. For example, at a business meeting, speaker after speaker talks in support of a motion. Some are silent; no one speaks against. You believe the motion is dangerous, even immoral. Do you speak, the lone voice against?

What enables this blind beggar—the "nobody" in the crowd, for sure—to speak up, despite loud voices raised to silence him? Perhaps, over the years, he's learned not to let his heart be silenced by inner voices of doubt, fear, disapproval. Perhaps his desire to see overcomes his fear. But Jesus names the deepest source of all: faith. His faith gave him the determination to speak, the will to jump when Jesus called.

Lord, give me faith to speak the truth of my heart, even when inner or outer voices want to silence me.

Mary Marrocco

One Step More

Seek good... Amos 5:14

Summer is a time for sharing our strawberries with neighbors, assisting family with tomato canning, treating children to heaping ice cream cones and even relaxing in mini-vacations with God and a spiritual book.

The prophet Amos, however, calls us not to just do good, but to seek good. The neighbor who irks us with an unkempt yard may have a back problem that she accepts without complaint. The elderly uncle who calls us late at night because he can't sleep perhaps rocked us to sleep as a baby. The daughter who is not going to church could be surrendering her difficult life to God's will in a quiet way.

During this season of picnics and porch swings, may we go one step beyond doing. May we seek the good in the life of each person we encounter and so discover God's reflection.

Sr. Bridget Haase, O.S.U.

Out of His Mind

He is out of his mind. Mark 3:21

What was it that got people talking this way about Jesus? Was he truly out of his mind? If we go by what Mark writes in this gospel passage, Jesus had days when his message ran up against conventional thinking. He did things and said things people thought were a little out there. Was it style or substance?

In a world of tribal hatred and blood vengeance, he told us to turn the other cheek. In a place where known sinners were to be shunned, he freely associated with them and engaged them in his ministry. At a time when the sick and lame were public outcasts, he touched their hearts and healed their wounds. Jesus was clearly out of his mind in love with a pathetic bunch of humans, so out of his mind he was willing to die for them and give them the gift of eternal life.

Paul Pennick

The Heart of the Matter

> Take my yoke upon you and learn from me, for I am meek and humble of heart; and you will find rest for yourselves.
>
> Matthew 11:29

For new parents—as well as grandparents, relations and friends—there's hardly a more thrilling moment than hearing that first heartbeat.

When that wooshing sound of life blood surging through a tiny body, pumped by a tiny heart, resounds in the room, we all breathe easier, we look at each other in wonder, and we might even laugh in delight.

It's the place of life and love—the heart. What a life that will grow, nourished by that beating heart, powered by it, sustained by it.

When we celebrate the Sacred Heart of Jesus, our Lord and brother, I reflect on his heart, beating not only with human life, but God's very life and love. Yes, I breathe easier and I might even laugh in delight and joy.

Jesus, bring me closer to your loving heart.

Amy Welborn

A Prayer for Salvation

I will make you a light to the nations,
that my salvation may reach to the ends of the earth.

Isaiah 49:6

When I hear the word "salvation," my first thought is of a kind of personal benefit, something that I or another person can claim and enjoy. But this passage from Isaiah suggests that God has another, larger view in which salvation is God's goal for all of creation. We may be privileged to play a part in that unfolding drama, if God so wills.

Strong convictions about our own salvation or about the Savior himself, then, are not meant to leave us self-satisfied. A certain degree of peace and joy naturally accompanies faith, but if God yearns for the salvation of the whole world, ought we not do the same? And if we do, what will that mean for our lives?

One thing it means, I think, is prayer for the salvation of other people, from those in our families to those in the far-flung places whose lives are unknown to us. May we also pray that in some mysterious way, our salvation might be linked to theirs.

Mark Neilsen

June 19

Allowing Ourselves to Feel

Harden not your hearts... Hebrews 3:8

The injunction, "harden not your hearts," is a frequent one in Scripture. It reminds us that God wants our hearts to be soft and sensitive to the movements of the Spirit and to the needs of others. How do we keep our hearts pliable?

First, we have to stay in touch with our own brokenness and pain. Mindful of our own wounds, we will be more apt to reach out to bind the wounds of others. Second, we must become more aware of individuals who need our help. We can offer to drive someone to the store or doctor, rent a documentary on human trafficking, serve at a homeless shelter, attend a talk on world hunger or babysit for busy parents. And third, we can do what you are doing right now: take a few minutes each day to reflect on the Scriptures, to focus on our faith and to ask God for help.

The American poet Archibald MacLeish wrote many years ago, "The crime against life...is not to feel." Allow yourself to feel today—and every day.

Sr. Melannie Svoboda, S.N.D.

One of Us

The child grew and became strong, filled with wisdom; and the favor of God was upon him. Luke 2:40

Does Jesus really understand your joys and your sorrows? When you lift up your burdens to him and ask for his help, does he understand what you are feeling? It might have been hard to say "yes" if Jesus had not fully shared in our human nature. But Jesus went through the stages of growth as we do, and he knew the joys and sorrows that are a part of every human life.

I think God always knew all about us because we are a part of his creation. But when God's Son took on our human nature, it became easier for us to believe that God understood who we are and what we feel.

Thank you, Jesus, for the great mercy you have shown by becoming fully one of us.

Fr. Kenneth Grabner, C.S.C.

A Voice in the Darkness

He woke up, rebuked the wind, and said to the sea, "Quiet! Be still!" Mark 4:39

Nature is amazing. As we peer down into the canyon, our voices bounce off rock walls like scattered pebbles. We are small. All the laws of science cannot capture the grandeur of what is real. Sometimes we disappear into events that break over us like a big wave.

The power of the sea is recognized even by those who live far from shifting tides. We hear how peoples crossed in small boats, many dying on the way. How they surely cried out for help. Like sailors, we learn to pray during storms.

Sometimes sleep is slow to reach us. Worry seems to churn all around. The darkness is real, and we cannot see far. But a presence is felt in the night. Troubles, like the sea, are bounded. We never make it through all by ourselves.

God, let us hear your voice in the darkness.

Jeanne Schuler

Order Out of Chaos

A mighty wind swept over the waters. Genesis 1:2

A story can be a wondrous container for a truth that must be told. The account in Genesis tells the truth of goodness in all creation. The creation story portrays the love of a creative God lifting beauty and order out of the chaos.

Be still and listen to the mighty wind sweeping over the dark waters. Imagine that the wind is the breath of God, the spirit of God. We have seen how the wind blows things out of old places into new places. Slowly the light and the darkness emerge. The waters separate; the sky becomes visible. The rhythm of day and night, morning and evening are revealed. The dry lands and the seas appear. And, oh, that marvelous moment when things begin to grow! The earth makes known her potential to produce fruits, vegetables and all kinds of plants—all because of the sun and the moon, the balance of light and darkness.

Loving Creator, in the midst of your creative work, you tell the truth of how good it is. Raise up grateful friends of the earth to sustain it.

Sr. Macrina Wiederkehr, O.S.B.

'They Prayed'

**Hearken, O Lord, to my prayer
and attend to the sound of my pleading.** Psalm 86:6

Some time ago I spent a week on a mission trip in Mexico, living among and working with young Catholic missionaries who prayed about everything. The van wouldn't start: They prayed. A wheat-intolerant missionary ate some of our tortillas: They prayed. My daughter's back started hurting: They prayed. We had trouble crossing the border: They prayed.

And every day, at every hour, people in need of help came to the door of the mission house. After offering what concrete help they could, of course, they prayed.

I don't know how it works. I don't know how God's action flows in and through our actions. But I do know this: We prayed.

Lord, deepen my prayer life as I come to you with all my needs.

Amy Welborn

DRAWN BY GOD

**My soul waits for the LORD
more than sentinels wait for the dawn.** Psalm 130:6

When sleep can't come, the night can seem endless. If you've accompanied and stood vigil with a loved one who's in pain, if you've kept watch waiting for a young driver to return home safely, if you've waited for an early morning phone call to assure you of a traveler's safe arrival, you know how longed for and how welcome daybreak is. Somehow, everything seems better in the light of day.

The psalmist tells us that these experiences reflect the deep hunger we have for God. Whether it's our own profound desire for the divine or the collective ache of our world for meaning and purpose, the yearning for God draws each of us.

Loving God, may the desire of my heart draw me closer to you this day.

Sr. Chris Koellhoffer, I.H.M.

COMING OUR WAY

The LORD will be passing by. 1 Kings 19:11

We are confident God is with us. Perhaps a gust of spiritual wind rushes through our bones, and we feel assured that we live in the Spirit. Sometimes the ground shifts beneath our feet, causing our hopes to sway and our dreams to totter. In these small earthquakes, we hold firm to our belief in divine assistance. Other times we may feel like we are living from the smoldering ashes of a religious fire that once was. But we know God understands our weakness.

As with Elijah in this reading, God also comes to us in tiny whispering sounds. Watching wild daisies dance in the sunlight, wiping water dripping from our child's face after a pool dive or eating watermelon together at a family gathering fills us with a sense of wonder and amazement at God's endless blessings and gracious gifts. In moments like these, we grasp that God is passing by, right here, right now. And we can only bow in reverence and gratitude.

Sr. Bridget Haase, O.S.U.

Faith Is Our Life

During the night, the angel of the Lord opened the doors of the prison, led them out, and said, "Go and take your place in the temple area, and tell the people everything about this life." Acts 5:19-20

As I prepared this devotion, I was struck by the words, "tell the people everything about this life." The phrase "this life" underscored for me that, for the early Christians, faith in Jesus was not a pastime, diversion or sport. It was their life. It was a commitment of their whole selves to the person and teachings of Jesus. As such, their faith formed their attitudes. It shaped their decision-making. It determined their choices. Sometimes their faith led them to prison or even to death in the public arena.

What about my faith? Is it a pastime, or is it central to my life? Is it a mere interest I have, or does it lie at the heart of who I am and all I do?

Jesus, may you and your teachings be at the core of who I am and all I do.

Sr. Melannie Svoboda, S.N.D.

Justice and Love

He loves justice and right. Psalm 33:5

Parents generally know how to mete out all kinds of just decisions on a daily basis. My sister gave me the tip on how to end disputes on who gets the biggest slice of pie: "Ok, child number one, you will cut the pie. And child number two, you will get first pick which piece is yours." It may not mean all parties are happy with the result, but it qualifies as justice in the family.

God's plan can also leave some of us unhappy with the results. We don't always get what we want. What might appear a fair solution for one party may hurt another. Our burdens can seem far heavier than those of our neighbor. Some will feel the sting of sharing what they don't wish to share. Some will enjoy the benefits of another's excess. True justice is fundamentally based on love. And where there is love, we will find God.

Paul Pennick

The Treasure That Is Friendship

**A faithful friend is a sturdy shelter;
he who finds one finds a treasure.** Sirach 6:14

Sirach's passage has surprisingly harsh comments about people we consider to be friends, warning that many are not to be trusted, that they will turn against us when things go wrong. But when we find a faithful friend, we have a great treasure.

Reading the passage made me think of treasured friendships in my life. People who have been with me through terrible times, who have showed up when I needed them most. They have worked with me, fed me, listened to me, prayed with me, sent me tickets, made me laugh. Held my foot sticking out of an MRI machine. Left a vacation to come help with grandchildren's head lice! Surprised me at the airport when I flew back late at night from my sister's funeral.

Victor Hugo wrote in *Les Miserables*, "To love another person is to see the face of God." Let us give thanks today for seeing God's face in friends.

Patricia Livingston

A Childlike Faith

Let the children come to me. Mark 10:14

It has to be one of our fondest childhood images of Jesus. Seated among a group of children, a smiling Jesus beckons the children to his side. We believed then what our parents told us, what Sister taught us and what Father said from the pulpit. This young man in the flowing robes with the kind face loved us and wanted us to be good, to help others, to pray and to love God. It seemed so simple then.

And yet in this same gospel, Jesus cautions us to retain a child-like faith if we are to enter heaven. There is nothing wrong in our search for rational explanations. God gave us that ability. But faith—the faith of a child—is based on love and trust and hope. It is that kind of faith that Jesus is asking us as grown-ups to retain from our youth. It's still a simple message of love of God and love of our neighbor. There is no need to complicate it, no pretense, no complex rationalizations. Jesus beckons the adults too.

Paul Pennick

Letting Go

We have given up everything and followed you. Mark 10:28

What moved Peter to say this? He'd just heard Jesus tell a rich young man to sell everything; the man went away, possessions intact, plus sadness. Perhaps Peter was eager to prove his superiority. Maybe he wanted to make sure all this sacrifice was going to get him somewhere. Possibly it was a backhanded complaint about hardships endured, or an indirect way of saying, "I'm scared but I'm with you." Peter could have been learning to tell Jesus, "I love you."

If I look inside myself, I find all these threads tangled up in my heart. In a movie I saw, a monk who owns nearly nothing watches sadly as his beautiful, beloved red blanket is taken away. He discovers he needs to let it go, as he's been putting it ahead of his love of Christ. I found it so hard to watch, and I realized that I, myself, have such attachments. If we let them, Jesus' words can illumine the shadowy places of our hearts.

My God! Help me to let go and let you in.

Mary Marrocco

CAN'T WE LISTEN?

They sent some Pharisees and Herodians to him to ensnare him in his speech. Mark 12:13

How much energy have I spent in my life trying to ensnare God in his speech?

Over and over in the Scriptures, in the prayer of the Church, in the witness of the saints, I see and hear that God loves me: that his love is lavish and passionate, that Christ loves so much that he died for me, that there is no logical reason for me to even be here, but that I and everyone else who exists are here on Earth simply because God loved us into existence.

Ah, we argue, that can't be. We seek evidence that God can't love us. We suffer, don't we? We fail. We're not deserving of love. We argue with God's words—his Word—and we try to ensnare him, to prove God wrong.

What would happen if I just stopped arguing?

Lord, I will listen.

Amy Welborn

Building Unity

> **You shall not bear hatred for your brother in your heart.**
> **Though you may have to reprove your fellow man, do not**
> **incur sin because of him.** Leviticus 19:17

Through Moses, God delivers these and other instructions for how the Israelite people are to treat each other. But they are just as useful for any group of people who are interested in preserving unity in their common life, a group like a church or a nation.

Hatred undermines the unity and solidarity that are essential for any community to survive. Yes, the Lord says, you may have to correct a sister or brother, but don't sin because of it.

Sin? I think the Lord means that "reprove" should not involve sarcasm, gossip, threats, carrying a grudge or the like. Offer your correction and then let the matter drop. Pray that the Holy Spirit will build unity for us around the truth.

Lord, help us to trust that the future is in your hands and not exclusively in ours.

Mark Neilsen

THE BLESSING OF WATER

For just as from the heavens
 the rain and snow come down...
So shall my word be... Isaiah 55:10-11

Water is a very apt image for God's word. Why? Water is essential for life. It is graceful and ungraspable. It also cleanses and rejuvenates. In fact, when Jesus spoke to the Samaritan woman at the well, he described his teachings as "living water." We can easily take the blessing of water for granted, especially if we have an adequate supply. Let us rekindle our reverence for water today by being mindful of every drop of water we use today—to drink, cook, wash or pour onto our plants. Then we can try to be more saving of the water we use. We can also educate ourselves on the water shortage in our world. And finally, we can take time just to be with water— whether an ocean, a lake, a pond, a stream, a fountain or even a single glassful—and give thanks to God for this great gift.

Gracious God, I thank you for the water of your Word and the water of planet Earth.

Sr. Melannie Svoboda, S.N.D.

All the Signs Are There

> Then some of the scribes and Pharisees said to him, "Teacher, we wish to see a sign from you." He said to them in reply, "An evil and unfaithful generation seeks a sign, but no sign will be given it except the sign of Jonah the prophet."
>
> Matthew 12:38-39

Perhaps Jesus thought those scribes and Pharisees had already received all the signs they needed. His teaching and his miracles were certainly sufficient to point out who he was. Those asking for signs had only to appreciate what had already been given.

When I think of all the signs of God's love in my life, I know that I have no need of more. He has shown his love by giving me the Eucharist and by guiding me through the inspirations of the Holy Spirit. He has surrounded me with caring friends and the beauty of his creation. I need no further signs, but I do need to appreciate more deeply the ones I already have.

Lord, may I not forget the many signs of your love that surround me each day.

Fr. Kenneth E. Grabner, C.S.C

Remembering the Past

> **By the streams of Babylon**
> **we sat and wept**
> **when we remembered Zion.** Psalm 137:1

This heartfelt lament is paired today with the stark account of Jerusalem's capture and the exile of its people. There is hardly a more deeply sad passage in all of the Hebrew Scriptures. The people felt far from God. The loss of Jerusalem felt like the end of everything. And while they were too bereft to sing praise to God, they were utterly determined to remember their past and their sacred city. They passed on what they remembered. Their descendants later returned "home" to a place they knew only through the memories of their elders. Centuries later, Jesus came to Jerusalem to die. For his followers, it felt like the end of everything. But once again, there was more to the story.

Spirit of God, you have been with believers throughout history. Be with me now!

Karla Manternach

Turnarounds Small and Great

They proclaimed a fast and all of them, great and small, put on sackcloth. Jonah 3:5

When we catch up with Jonah, he's already had the experience of running from God's command and being thrown overboard, only to be swallowed by a large fish. In this Scripture story, once was enough for Jonah. When God commanded him a second time to go to Nineveh and preach repentance, he went with haste and without hesitation.

To their credit, the people of Nineveh listened, and listened well. Whether the motivation was Jonah's sharing the tale of his harrowing experience and the consequences of his refusing to obey God, we don't know. What the Scriptures do tell us is that the entire city, including the king, immediately entered into prayer and fasting and made a significant change in their lifestyle.

So it is with us. Genuine transformation begins with deep listening to God at work in our lives and then entering into radical turnaround in ways large and small.

Sr. Chris Koellhoffer, I.H.M.

'Grown-Up' Christians

Do not think that I have come to abolish the law or the prophets. I have come not to abolish but to fulfill. Matthew 5:17

A friend of mine always tells her daughters to "put your big girl pants on" and face the hard things of life. In a sense, and with a great deal more delicacy, this is what Jesus is asking us to do. What he says here so simply is something that, when we begin to understand it, marks a passage into maturity of spiritual development. He is talking about that shift that each of us must make in our faith journey that calls us to be "grown-up" Christians. Radical fundamentalist interpretation of God's law as revealed to Moses and the prophets is fulfilled in the spirit of the law, revealed by Jesus and gifted to us through his Holy Spirit. God speaks to hearts that seek him solely. Listening deeply to Jesus in word and sacrament, we come to understand that he does not abolish what we once clung to, but that he invites us to trust him in prayer to experience more fully and with greater fidelity the "freedom of the children of God."

Claire J. King

Worry Less, Trust More

Do not worry about tomorrow; tomorrow will take care of itself. Matthew 6:34

Life is full of things to worry about: relationships, job security, finances, health, world peace, the health of the planet. We want to protest, "But, Jesus, we must worry about tomorrow. We must plan, save and prepare for the days and years ahead!"

I doubt we will ever eradicate all worry, and I doubt Jesus is dismissing all prudent planning for the future. But we can prevent it from being the driving force of our lives, and his words challenge us to loosen the grip we have as we strive (in vain) to be "in complete control." Prepare, yes, but be open to surprise. Plan, yes, but be flexible. Save, yes, but always be generous to those in need, trusting that God will somehow bless our giving.

Bottom line: God loves us more than we can imagine and will ultimately provide all we really need in life. Honest.

Loving God, teach me to worry less and trust you more.

Sr. Melannie Svoboda, S.N.D.

Prayer of the Word

For just as from the heavens
   the rain and snow come down
And do not return there
   till they have watered the earth,
   making it fertile and fruitful...
So shall my word be
   that goes forth from my mouth;
It shall not return to me void,
   but shall do my will,
   achieving the end for which I sent it. Isaiah 55:10-11

O God, may I always and everywhere listen to your word, reverence it, cherish it, nurture it—and never hinder it from doing its work of striving to make me more genuinely holy.

Billions of human words crowd the airwaves each day. Billions more are printed each day, nearly all of them trying to sell, to entertain, to inform—and, at times, to confuse or even deceive. I could easily drown in this daily flood of words.

Your word, O God, is not like a screaming verbal vortex. Your word is like the soft rain and melting snow that quietly penetrates and slowly nourishes. Your word comes, not in noisy fanfare, irritating shouts and information overload, but rather in silence and in restful peace.

May your word, O God, be ever more fruitful in me. Help me to do my part so that the goal you want to achieve in me with your word is realized.

James E. Adams

WE BOW IN WORSHIP

Come, let us bow down in worship;
let us kneel before the LORD who made us. Psalm 95:6

As a young man, before I became Catholic, I found the "calisthenics" of the Catholic liturgy puzzling. I couldn't understand all the bowing and kneeling. Why would God require all the "ups and downs," I wondered? The ritual of movement within the Mass was beyond my comprehension, so I dismissed it as extraneous to true faith and belief.

But as I grew in understanding and experienced the grace of the Eucharist, I embraced these simple movements as the foundations of prayer that prepared me for the sometimes difficult work of meeting God. For when I kneel and cross myself, I am reminded that I am entering holy ground and time—a space set apart especially for my communion with God. I lower myself in order to be elevated to God.

Father, see me kneel before you.

Steve Givens

Change of Direction

> [Jesus] said to them, "Thus it is written that the Messiah would suffer and rise from the dead on the third day and that repentance, for the forgiveness of sins, would be preached in his name to all the nations…" Luke 24:46-47

The word "repent" is sometimes rendered as "a change of direction." Sometimes it is only an experience of spiritual starvation that can wake us up to our predicament and lead us to turn our lives around. In extreme cases, repentance might well involve some pretty intense feelings of shame, guilt and even fear. Should an experience of forgiveness follow, the experience of joy and release might be similarly intense.

But even those who are trying to follow Christ faithfully can feel ashamed, guilty and afraid—sometimes even afraid of admitting their sin. By changing direction, perhaps toward the Sacrament of Reconciliation, we can always experience the forgiveness of sins that Jesus came to offer us.

Mark Neilsen

Trust in the Risen Christ

Just as Moses lifted up the serpent in the desert, so must the Son of Man be lifted up, so that everyone who believes in him may have eternal life. John 3:14-15

For the fourth Gospel, a narrative about Moses in the Hebrew Scriptures foreshadows Jesus' being "lifted up" on the cross; only here we are to "believe in him" in order to "have eternal life."

The word John uses for "believe" does not mean to accept something as real with no evidence for doing so, with no experience upon which to base our belief. Rather, it means to trust in the risen Christ in the context of the ongoing experience of a relationship with him in the faith community called "Church."

Lord Jesus, help me to give myself entirely to trusting in you in all things.

Mitch Finley

Love and Wrath

Whoever believes in the Son has eternal life, but whoever disobeys the Son will not see life, but the wrath of God remains upon him. John 3:36

In the New Testament, we hear so much more about God's love than his wrath. That's really an Old Testament word, isn't it?

We know the stories: Adam and Eve felt God's wrath when they disobeyed God's command, the Israelites spent time in bondage in Egypt and Babylon, Jonah saw the world from inside a fish's belly when he tried to disobey God.

But the stories of God's immeasurable love are more familiar still to us: multiplying the loaves and fishes, raising Lazarus from the dead, healing the woman with a hemorrhage.

John reminds us here, however, that God requires obedience to our covenant with him. There is no equivocating in his language. We are called to believe in the Son, to love and serve the Father as he did, and to love our neighbors as ourselves. No small task.

Heather Wilson

Failure Transformed

A scribe approached and said to him, "Teacher, I will follow you wherever you go." Matthew 8:19

Marriage vows are now often preserved on videotape, leaving a concrete reminder of one's promises. When those promises are broken through infidelity or some other failure, the video reminder must be heart-wrenching.

When we are young, we find it relatively easy to make sweeping promises, but as we age, our initial enthusiasm often wanes and our commitments lose their appeal. We may discover that some of what we did in the name of Jesus was driven more by fear than faith.

We are in good company. After proclaiming his complete faithfulness, Peter failed miserably and experienced the kind of self-knowledge that purifies us of self-righteousness and reminds us that, as Dorothy Day said, "all is grace." Peter was transformed because grace and repentance came together to allow him to experience a love that was not conditional and a forgiveness that was not earned. May our wounds become a source of healing for others.

Mark Neilsen

'DO NOT BE AFRAID'

It is I. Do not be afraid. John 6:20

What a story! Jesus' disciples pile into a boat, in the dark, and push off onto the sea. A few miles out, Jesus comes walking across the water, which scares the living daylights out of everyone—understandably. But we may take this at more than face value. Take it as representing any unexpected or frightening experience you might have; unexpected, frightening news about your health; scary news about someone you love; anything like this. Know that even when something frightens you, even in that news, in that experience, the Lord Jesus is present in the middle of it. Yes, it can be scary when he arrives in an unexpected way. But he is there, and he speaks, "It is I. Do not be afraid." Over and over, quietly, confidently, he whispers in your heart, "It is I. Do not be afraid. Do not be afraid. Do not be afraid. It is I."

Lord Jesus, help me to recognize you when you come in unexpected ways.

Mitch Finley

RECALLING WHAT GOD HAS DONE

**Hear now, all you who fear God, while I declare
what he has done for me.** Psalm 66:16

In my weakest moments, when fear threatens to engulf me and my unbelief taunts me, I recall how God has saved me in the past.

I have a list of these intimate miracles—when God has gone before me and turned an impossible situation around, when circumstances were so aligned against me that the presence of an Almighty God was the only explanation remaining after the dust settled. I recall when I had a hiding place in a storm, when my heart was gently placed on the other side of a cavern. He has prevailed on my behalf; he has never abandoned or forsaken me in my need, no matter how unworthy I felt at the time. When I speak these memories out loud, something shifts. The heavens open in response to my praise, and my heart opens in response to his power.

Kristin Armstrong

GOD IS ALWAYS FOR US

God will wipe away every tear from their eyes. Revelation 7:17

This comforting Scripture verse implies a lot. Often used at funeral services, the message is not only for those who mourn. Anyone who has a tough life, who suffers from physical, emotional, mental or spiritual pain, can find solace in a tender God who cares enough to wipe away tears. This tender gesture assures us that no matter how terrible the suffering is, there will come a time, either in this life or the next, when suffering will be no more. Not only will every tear be wiped away, each one will be held in the compassionate embrace of a God who is always for us and never against us. This promise enables us to hold hope in our hearts and to trust in God's compassionate presence in spite of whatever weighs us down.

Tender-hearted One, I bring the tears of each suffering person to you today. Wipe away their tears and assure them of your unfailing kindness and care.

Sr. Joyce Rupp, O.S.M.

Finding God in Ordinary Moments

Blessed day by day be the Lord,
who bears our burdens; God, who is our salvation.

Psalm 68:20

While on my first retreat, the retreat leader asked us to recall the moments in our life when we felt most loved. I immediately thought of the time my mother carried me several blocks home from a Fourth of July fireworks display. I was five years old and had been so terrified by the loud noises that I begged to leave. I recalled feeling utterly safe and secure as I drifted in and out of sleep in the arms of my mother as she made what must have been a difficult trip back home.

As wonderful and awe-inspiring as mystical experiences of the Divine might be, I have learned that it is the ability to recognize God's presence in the ordinary moments of life that carry us through.

Lord, help us recognize the many ways you come to us each day.

Terri Mifek

Bearing a Rich Harvest

> But the seed sown on rich soil is the one who hears the word and understands it, who indeed bears fruit and yields a hundred or sixty or thirtyfold. Matthew 13:23

These words are consoling to me because the results of my life often fall short of a hundredfold. After I've done my best, my yield sometimes falls within the sixty or thirtyfold range. If I have truly done my best, that is okay because then I will have used my gifts to the best of my ability.

We have a gracious God who accepts us as we are. God knows our limitations. If we do the best with what we have been given, then we will become the people God created us to be.

Lord, help me to be satisfied with the amount of fruit I have been able to bear for you and for others. May I not compare myself to others whom I think are more gifted than I. Help me to be grateful for my gifts and for all that you have enabled me to accomplish.

Fr. Kenneth E. Grabner, C.S.C.

A Ministry of Encouragement

They sent Barnabas [to go] to Antioch. When he arrived and saw the grace of God, he rejoiced and encouraged them all to remain faithful to the Lord in firmness of heart, for he was a good man, filled with the holy Spirit and faith. Acts 11:22-24

Because of the persecution of the believers in Jerusalem, a number of Jesus' followers ended up in Antioch where the Holy Spirit was cultivating a new kind of church, one that would include both Jews and Gentiles. The Church leaders in Jerusalem sent Barnabas to go and check it out. Barnabas' journey of almost 400 miles covered far less ground than the gigantic leap of faith it must have taken for him to open his heart to the possibility that the spirit of Jesus was moving in a new way in Antioch, yet he chose to respond with encouragement.

What if we were to take up the "Ministry of Encouragement" today, purposely looking for what's going right and taking the time to affirm it? Can we open our eyes and hearts today to all the strengths and virtues present in ourselves, in others, in the workplace, in our community and country?

Claire J. King

Turning to God

Do not let your hearts be troubled. John 14:1

Do you remember the situation in which Jesus urged his disciples to not let their hearts be troubled? It was shortly before the worst experience of their lives: witnessing the Passion and death of their beloved leader and friend. This same message is offered to us in our times of trial and tribulation. This does not mean that feelings of anxiety and dread will cease to arise in us if we have faith in Jesus' words. Rather, when we take his message to heart, we do not let these feelings get the best of us. We keep turning toward our Friend with confidence, trusting that we will have strength to endure and make it through the rocky terrain of our troubles.

Dear Friend of my heart, when I am troubled, draw me to you. Remind me that you are near.

Sr. Joyce Rupp, O.S.M.

THE NEED FOR HUMILITY

The Father who dwells in me is doing his works. John 14:10

I once read that pride was near the top of the list as far as sin is concerned. I first read that many years ago and have come across it many times since. Among other things, pride is a severely inflated ego. We feel quite at home assuming that we are in control of our lives and that we are capable of figuring out all things. Then we fall on our faces and need help. And in that fall comes life's most important lesson: God is within us accomplishing his work. We need the humility to allow him a growing presence in our lives. Jesus was humble—he looked on all he had as a gift, a gift that he shares with us. Pride indeed comes before the fall. But when we rise, we do so with God's help, asking that he be there when we fall again.

Fr. James Stephen Behrens, O.C.S.O.

An Apostolic Faith

Hold fast to the word I preached to you... 1 Corinthians 15:2

Paul goes on to recount the word he preaches: that Christ died for our sins, was buried, was raised and appeared to Peter and the twelve and others—some still living, some now dead.

This isn't a mystical, ethereal word, but a tangible, visible one. Its power is in this: These things really happened on our own earth, to real people whose names we know. These apostles were eyewitnesses of the resurrection. Our Christian faith is apostolic because it's rooted in the witness of the apostles.

Paul never met the historical Jesus, but he claims apostleship because Christ "appeared to me." The apostles' witness is not exterior to us; it's corroborated by the presence of the risen Christ in our own hearts. That's why we, too, have an "apostolate" to witness and proclaim the resurrection. We do so with all the apostles in the Easter light we experience this very day.

Mary Marrocco

A CAUSE FOR JOY

I have told you this so that my joy may be in you and your joy may be complete. John 15:11

The joy of friendship grows when people share the values that make them who they are. The greater the sharing, the greater the joy. That's the way friendship works, and if I reflect on my friendships, I can better understand Jesus' words in the gospel.

It was a joy for Jesus to share his word with the people of his time, just as it is a joy for him to do so with us. We hear his word through the Scriptures and through his Spirit that speaks in our hearts. Jesus' love prompts him to share his values with us, and if we make them a part of our lives, we begin to resemble the mind and heart of Jesus. What a cause for joy!

Thank you, Lord, for the joy you give me through the revelation of your love, and thank you for my ability to bring joy to you through my acceptance of your word.

Fr. Kenneth Grabner

Bringing What Is Most Needed

[They] brought great joy to all the brothers. Acts 15:3

It's strange how joy and suffering can be present at the same time. Recently, I spoke with Laila, a woman who'd long been in a troubled marriage that included violence and deceit. As often happens, her children's pain, rather than her own, woke her up to the need for change. The first change she made was to go deep within and discover the strength of God's love there, his particular love for her. "He loves each one of us as though there were only one of us," St. Augustine wrote. Even amid anguish, Laila discovered the joy of being loved by God as though she were the only one.

We needn't wait until things are fine to claim such joy. It's here, waiting to be picked up like a child and played with. It's attractive. In our world of overabundance, there's no better way to be noticed than to be joyful. Joy draws all. When the apostles brought joy to the sisters and brothers, they brought what was most needed. So can we.

Mary Marrocco

A Prosperity of the Soul

**The father of orphans and the defender of widows
is God in his holy dwelling.** Psalm 68:6

There are late-night televangelists who preach a "gospel of prosperity." They promise (especially if you send a donation) that if your faith in God is strong enough, you will be blessed in ways that will make you successful and powerful. While I have no doubt that God can work through us in any way he chooses, I don't believe that the "power of my faith" affects my wealth and social standing.

What God can and does give us is an inner peace based on what we really need. Our strength in life comes not from telling God to give us what we think we need, but rather from depending on God to give us our daily bread. My life is good. I think I have all that I need and then some. But I glory in the fact that my God is also the God of orphans, widows and the poor—those who might have less but who receive the same measure of inner peace and strength that only God can deliver.

God, be the provider of prosperity for my soul.

Steve Givens

Jesus Prays for Us

I do not pray for the world but for the ones you have given me... John 17:9

This statement sounds surprisingly exclusive for Jesus, the one who shared supper with sinners and had friendships with women. But this long prayer is aimed primarily at his disciples whose real work of discipleship would begin after Jesus' death. He knew they would need to believe that he and God were with them in the dark days that would follow.

Since I chose the path of faith and have sought to become a disciple of Jesus, I take comfort in considering myself among the ones Jesus prayed for. But the threats I face are almost opposite those encountered by the first disciples. Instead of the danger of dying for my beliefs, I face the danger of complacency in this Christianity-dominated culture. When I wonder if going to Mass and praying really matters, it helps me to know that Jesus prayed for me to persevere.

Aileen A. O'Donoghue

Allowing Jesus to Instruct Us

I have come to believe that you are the Messiah, the Son of God, the one who is coming into the world. John 11:27

The speaker is Martha, the woman whom Jesus had earlier admonished for being "anxious and worried about many things" (Luke 10:41). Apparently she took his words to heart, for at this point in John's Gospel, she is clear and forthright. She knows who Jesus really is.

Like Peter, who similarly affirmed Jesus as the Messiah (Mark 8:29), Martha has her ups and downs in the gospels. She has gone through a transformation in her relationship with Jesus: at first she had a definite idea of how Jesus ought to act like a Messiah, next came Jesus' response, and finally she grew in faith as a result of listening to what the Lord had said.

For all of us who have wrongly expected God to fulfill our every expectation, Martha is a source of great encouragement. The question is: Can we let Jesus instruct us, even if he is a little blunt at times, and take his words to heart? If so, there is hope for us, for Jesus now and always has the words of eternal life.

Lord, help me to come to believe in you with all my heart.

Mark Neilsen

Recognizing God's Power

> Show forth, O God, your power,
> the power, O God, with which you took our part.
>
> Psalm 68:29

I have felt God's divine power many times during my life. I have felt it during those "high holy days" when God seems most present, such as my wedding and the birth of my children. I have felt that power surge through me while standing on the rim of the Grand Canyon and while listening to a majestic piece of music in a massive and ornate symphony hall.

But I have also felt the seeming utter absence of God's power as I have watched loved ones die or as I have struggled with my own health challenges. Faith doesn't mean we will always feel the power of God in our lives. But faith does mean that we will somehow find the strength—even in the midst of our greatest weaknesses—to shout, "Where are you God?" That cry to the heavens, even if it seems to be made in a moment of little faith, is actually a moment of great belief that God is present and listening.

God, never let me forget those moments when I have seen your power.

Steve Givens

Courage in Darkness

You will not abandon my soul to the nether world…

Psalm 16:10

My father died years ago. In the month he spent in hospitals enduring procedures that ultimately failed, I often found myself reciting this phrase like a mantra, alternating between "his soul" and "my soul." It helped me believe that the discomforts and indignities of dad's final days were not going to be his ultimate end.

I didn't always believe the words of the psalm, but I clung to them like a small flashlight trying to illuminate the dark, descending stairway on the journey of life. In truth, I would have rather turned and fled back up the stairs into my youth. But, alas, the arrow of time forbids that. So I wrapped my hands tightly around my flashlight of words, seeking the courage to continue stepping into the future.

Aileen A. O'Donoghue

A DAZZLING REVELATION

> [Jesus] was transfigured before them, and his clothes became dazzling white… Then a cloud came, casting a shadow over them. Mark 9:2-3, 7

This strange event seems to cover the full range of human experience: the ordinary muddle, the crystal clarity and the downright puzzling. Jesus in his divinity is revealed alongside Moses and Elijah, those iconic representations of the Law and the Prophets. But no sooner does that happen than the cloud descends, obscuring what had just been revealed. Just like that, our certainties elude us the moment we think we've figured it all out.

God, the Transfiguration seems to say, is as present in the dazzling Christ as in the obscuring cloud, in the clarity of understanding as in the confusion of mind.

But revealed in the most dramatic moments of our lives, God is no less present in the ordinary awareness of every single day. Jesus goes down the mountain with the disciples, more than ever convinced that in certainty or confusion and everything in between, he is with them.

Lord, reveal yourself to me today.

Mark Neilsen

Responding to the Call

> "Lord, you know everything; you know that I love you." [Jesus] said to him, "Feed my sheep." John 21:17

I once saw a child throwing a tantrum outside a grocery store because, evidently, his mother wouldn't give him the candy bar he wanted. His mother rightly said, "I love you, but you're not getting that candy bar." He continued to wail all the way to the car. I'm sure that four-year-old loved his mother, but he had not yet learned that true love requires a response. When we love, we must be willing to respond to the needs of the other. A parent needs to be obeyed.

The same holds true of our relationship with God. If we say we love God but are unwilling to respond to what he asks of us, what good is our love? God's desire is that we love him and care for those around us. We don't get to choose just one of those things. It's a package deal, and our required response is a resounding, "Yes, I will do what you ask of me."

Lord, give me the courage and the strength to respond to your call.

Steve Givens

When Your Heart Isn't in It

The Lord searches the just and the wicked. Psalm 11:5

Believing that God knows my motives is both a comforting and a frightening thought. On the one hand, when I put my heart and soul into things that flop, it comforts me to think that I might get some credit for the sincerity of the effort. But when I feel insincere, being nice to someone I don't really care for or "going through the motions" of a ritual I'm finding meaningless, I don't want to be known so deeply. I feel like a fraud at those times and would prefer to keep my deceit to myself.

I suppose it is in doing good deeds—even when my heart isn't in it, when I'm acting against my preferences—that I'm living out Jesus' demand to love my neighbor. So I keep practicing doing right in spite of feeling like a fraud and pray that my heart may someday follow my actions.

Aileen A. O'Donoghue

Moving Beyond Sadness

Jesus, looking at him, loved him and said to him, "...Go, sell what you have, and give to [the] poor..." Mark 10:21

Sometimes Scripture shocks us with words that come from a strange place. What could they mean? How could we sell all and give to the poor and follow Jesus? If Jesus told us to strap on a load and climb a mountain, at least we would know how to bend under burdens.

The rich man wants eternal life with God. He has followed the law and been faithful. But Jesus wants one more thing. The rich man is crushed and goes away sad. Even Jesus' disciples are upset by the story. Who has the strength to be saved?

Jesus looks on us with love. Faced with weakness and need, we turn away too soon. We hear only about the loss, but not about the promise. Jesus promises treasure. Our lives are not empty in his presence. We are not alone. On the path beyond fear and holding tight to things, our load strangely lightens.

God, free me from the sadness that I have to go it alone.

Jeanne Schuler

WELCOMING ALL WARMLY

Be hospitable to one another without complaining. 1 Peter 4:9

I wonder if it is easier to be more hospitable to a stranger than it is to welcome those who are with us on a regular basis. After all, strangers come and go. Family members, coworkers and religious community members are with us daily. They bring their moods, opinions and distasteful quirks. These people can sorely challenge our willingness to receive them with an open mind and heart. And here's the cruncher: We are to be hospitable "without complaining."

How do we overcome our natural inclination of wanting to turn away and close the door of love to them? How do we move our hearts to extend hospitable kindness? Peter supplies the answer to this dilemma several verses later: "Whoever serves, let it be with the strength that God supplies" (verse 11). Genuine hospitality toward those who sometimes drive us crazy only happens when we draw on divine strength!

Today I will be aware of those I welcome warmly and those on whom I shut the door.

Sr. Joyce Rupp, O.S.M.

Growing in Spirituality

I have much more to tell you, but you cannot bear it now.

John 16:12

I've often wondered what Jesus intended to tell his apostles but did not because they were not ready to hear it. Why were they unable to bear it at that time? He revealed to them concepts of the Most Holy Trinity, the Holy Eucharist and numerous teachings through parables. He told them at least three times of his coming death and resurrection. Perhaps they did not comprehend the real messages. Perhaps when they were more advanced in spirituality, the deeper meaning of his words would be understood.

The same may be true for us. We may hear many religious teachings but not fully internalize them because we still have to develop spiritually. Through the gift of faith, we can grow in our understanding of divine truths, dispose ourselves to accept God's deeper mysteries.

Jesus, I open my life to your teachings. Help me grow spiritually.

Fr. James McKarns

A Model for Us All

She, from her poverty, has contributed all she had, her whole livelihood. Mark 12:44

Have you ever noticed how Jesus seems to be toughest on those who get lost in the letter of the law? He admonishes teachers in positions of authority and power not to get stuck in petty, legalistic, external practices and forget the more authentic places of the heart. In one of William Stafford's poems, "The Little Ways That Encourage Good Fortune," the poet sounds a bit like Jesus in cautioning folks who are trying to make things right in the lives of others yet do not have things right in their own lives. Let's take that to our hearts for pondering.

Perhaps it is because the motive behind our actions is so crucial that Jesus holds up the poor widow as a shining light, a model for us all. Her two small coins are symbols not of wealth and prestige but of immense love. Jesus wants us to notice that.

Lord, help me be attentive to the motives behind my actions today.

Sr. Macrina Wiederkehr, O.S.B.

A Feast Spread Before Us

Five loaves and two fish are all we have, unless we ourselves go and buy food for all these people. Luke 9:13

We humans usually are unaware of God's designs. The disciples decide they have a problem: 5,000 people who have been listening to Jesus' preaching are hungry, and it's getting late. Solution: Send them away, for certainly the apostles shouldn't be expected to provide for them themselves. Imagine the shopping trip that would require, the money! I can imagine them thinking, "We are tired, too, and hungry."

This is what I call "stingy thinking," and I am guilty of it myself. Instead of approaching a situation from the perspective of what God might do, I approach it from what I alone would do—or don't want to do. These situations become problems. For God, there is no problem. Because God is love, he gives himself, as Jesus at the last Supper provided his Church with his Body and Blood for food and drink. He foresaw our hunger and thirst and spread a feast before us.

Sr. Kathryn James Hermes, F.S.P.

Transformed by Jesus' Words

Jesus then said to the Twelve, "Do you also want to leave?" Simon Peter answered him, "Master, to whom shall we go? You have the words of eternal life." John 6:67-68

The alternatives are many, as anyone who has ever seriously considered finding something to take the place of Jesus knows. Not only are there other religions and other teachers, many are the distractions and obsessions that can draw on our mental and physical resources. Those alternatives may not have eternal life, but in the meantime, they can be quite absorbing.

If we count ourselves among those who, like Peter, can't imagine anywhere else to go, that doesn't quite settle the matter either. Jesus asks about our hearts, about what we want. If we stay but really want to leave, then we stay halfheartedly. We remain lukewarm, Christian in name only.

If, on the other hand, we really believe Jesus has the words of eternal life, then we will be transformed by those words into genuine disciples and drawn into full union with Christ.

Lord, make a wholehearted believer out of me.

Mark Neilsen

With All Your Heart...

> Therefore, you shall love the LORD, your God, with all your heart, and with all your soul, and with all your strength.
>
> Deuteronomy 6:5

Sometimes we don't give it our all. We nod without really listening when our spouse wants to go over vacation plans yet again. We fail to take our usual care with an assignment at work, figuring what we've done is "good enough." We make a mental grocery list instead of truly listening and reflecting during the homily. It's not that we've done anything disruptive or evil; we're just not totally there.

But halfheartedness doesn't work with God. He calls on us to show our love with every thought, word and action, not just when we want or need something. God wants our fully engaged presence all the time. He desires nothing less than our whole heart—because that's what he gives us every day in every way.

Lord, I humbly ask that you help me show my love for you at all times.

Melanie Rigney

OUT OF THE DARKNESS

Many rebuked him, telling him to be silent. But he kept calling out all the more... Mark 10:48

On hearing that Jesus was near, the blind beggar shouted out. Like a noisy child, he was told to be quiet, but he did not listen. Jesus heard his shouting above the crowd and called him. The man jumped up when he heard his name.

Like children as they grow, we learn to be quiet. Feelings are formed, goals are clarified, and desires are tamed. Our knowledge swells, but some questions we once wondered about are set aside. In this corner we place our brokenness and the desire for something more.

Like Bartimaeus by the side of the road, we want to see. We want lives that make sense and questions hidden in our hearts to cry out again. We want healing. It was not in resignation that the blind man found healing. He did not hide his darkness. He did not forget himself. He shouted.

God, hear me and let me hear you in the darkness.

Jeanne Schuler

Nothing Left But Love

What man among you having a hundred sheep and losing one of them would not leave the ninety-nine in the desert and go after the lost one until he finds it? Luke 15:4

I saw my friend a month before she died. The cancer she had been battling for years was finally winning; she had stopped treatment and was preparing. She was ready, she said, but still a little afraid. One thing she wasn't afraid of, she said, was Purgatory.

"I want to go to Purgatory," she said. "I want to have everything purified until nothing but love is left." After leaving, I was confronted with the question of my own inner life. Do I want to be purified? What am I hanging on to and keeping from God's embrace? What part of me am I hiding deep in the hills, pretending to be lost, hoping not to be found, even by the One who is nothing but love?

Jesus, find me.

Amy Welborn

This Is It

> I live, no longer I, but Christ lives in me; insofar as I now live in the flesh, I live by faith in the Son of God who has loved me and given himself up for me. Galatians 2:20

If you were looking for a Bible verse that sums up Christianity in a sentence, you have it here. The Jesus who loved me so much that he gave his life to save mine lives in the depths of my being. Now he, not me, is the living center of my life. My life comes to me today as a gift of God as I live it in union with Jesus living in me. That is the awesome reality. To discover it for oneself is what Christianity is all about.

Perhaps you are acquainted with the "Jesus Prayer." It is short and simple: "Lord Jesus Christ, Son of God, have mercy on me, a sinner." Many Christians pray it repeatedly throughout the day. To a young monk who asked how he could be transformed by Christ, an older monk replied, "Go into your room and keep praying the Jesus prayer from your heart. The prayer will do the rest."

I dare say the same is true of Paul's statement. Go into your heart; keep pondering these words. Jesus in you will do the rest.

Kevin Perrotta

The Sound of Altruism

When you give alms, do not blow a trumpet before you...

Matthew 6:2

I used to give to a charity that made a point of not being a part of the nonprofit, tax-deductible system. I'm not sure of all their reasons, but I knew they worked with the poorest of the poor in our city, and I admired them for that. I would haul old clothes, household goods and food up to their inner-city location several times a year. They never took my name; they never put me on a mailing list; they never bothered me at all. It was a completely anonymous exchange, no fanfare whatsoever.

Then for some reason—probably inconvenience—I stopped making the trip. We began to give our used goods to tax-deductible organizations. They pick up our offering from our front door, leave a card for "tax purposes" and follow up a few weeks later with a phone call to schedule another pickup. It is so efficient, so easy.

Quietly, faintly, when we fill out the IRS forms each year, I think I hear a trumpet blowing.

Paul Pennick

HAIL MARY!

Mary set out and traveled to the hill country in haste to a town of Judah, where she entered the house of Zechariah and greeted Elizabeth. Luke 1:39-40

What an amazing woman: young, accepting the angel's promise of an unmarried pregnancy that would result in a Savior, and oh so quickly visiting her older cousin, also miraculously pregnant, to serve God's will in that birth too.

Then, centuries later, mindful of her life of humble, vulnerable and compassionate service, the Church makes an infallible declaration that, at the end of her life, God immediately welcomed Mary, body and soul, into the kingdom of heaven.

Occasionally, there is an additional twist and the Assumption is not a holy day of obligation. It is rather a holy day of opportunity. Like Mary freely visiting and caring for her cousin, you may want, freely and without obligation, to celebrate the Eucharist with your parish community. You may also, like Mary, want to visit—literally or by phone or mail—someone in need in order to assist them.

Hail Mary, full of grace, the Lord is with you...

Fr. James Krings

Who Are My Heroes?

How awesome you are, Elijah! Whose glory is equal to yours?

Sirach 48:4

The Book of Sirach contains eulogies to some of Israel's greatest heroes. The prophet Elijah is praised for his passionate rhetoric and miraculous powers.

Today might be a good day to ask myself who my heroes are, who are the ones I admire. Perhaps I admire a parent, a son, a daughter, a friend, a colleague or a neighbor. Maybe it's someone in the public arena: an athlete, an entertainer, a political leader, a church member or a historic figure.

The next question to ask myself would be why I admire these individuals, what qualities do they possess that attract me. Is it merely fame, fortune or power, or is it something far deeper like integrity, tenderheartedness, fortitude, courage or devotion to a worthy cause? To what extent is Jesus my hero? Remember, in the long run, our heroes reflect who we are and the values we hold dear.

Loving God, direct my attention to heroes who can inspire and encourage me along the road of life.

Sr. Melannie Svoboda, S.N.D.

August 16

Many Crowns

...be examples to the flock. And when the chief Shepherd is revealed, you will receive the unfading crown of glory.

1 Peter 5:3-4

Who doesn't want an "unfading crown of glory"? Sounds pretty great. But do we want to go through what it takes to get one?

In this address to early Christians, Peter is asking them to live as Jesus lived, to "be examples" of Christ. No easy task, then or now.

However, striving to live as Christ did, while difficult, is truly joyful. When we do so, we receive crowns here and now. Look around and you will find them: your children, your spouse, your prayer for a friend, a hard day's work, your kindness to a stranger. Our accomplishments, when undertaken in the spirit of furthering God's kingdom, are glorious.

King of Kings, help me to see the good that I have achieved and to aspire to do more, for your greater glory.

Terence Hegarty

Asking a Lot

So be perfect... Matthew 5:48

If I take Jesus seriously, his words are profoundly disturbing. Be perfect? Me? Jesus is asking the impossible—and not leaving room for anything less. He makes it clear that only perfection will be good enough. Given who Jesus is, I can't walk away from his words. Yet given who I am, I can't conceive of ever meeting the demand.

Obviously Jesus conceives of it. But by what process does he conceive it can happen? And, to put it in practical terms, what am I supposed to do to cooperate with this process of perfection, whose goal is inconceivable to me?

The answer lies in the rest of his summons: "Be perfect, just as your heavenly Father is perfect." The God whose perfection Jesus calls me to imitate is my Father. And so, while the road from here to perfection stretches beyond the horizon, I can walk on it today because my Father is with me on the road. He will never abandon me. He will accompany me along the road, at the rate I can go, until he brings me home, perfected, to himself.

Kevin Perrotta

Recommitting Ourselves to Christ

[Jesus] asked them, "Who do the crowds say that I am?" They said in reply, "John the Baptist; others, Elijah; still others, 'One of the ancient prophets has arisen.'" Then he said to them, "But who do you say that I am?" Peter said in reply, "The Messiah of God." Luke 9:18-20

Peter was the first disciple to profess that Jesus was the Messiah. Even though he was impulsive and imperfect, Peter could still see clearly that Jesus was uniquely important. He denied that importance later, even denied his own friend. But rather than crumple and abandon his faith altogether, he renewed his commitment to Jesus and proclaimed to the world that Jesus was the Messiah. Our own faith is imperfect like Peter's. We sin. We fail. Can we also summon the courage to begin again, to recommit ourselves to Christ, to remember who Jesus is?

Lord Jesus, you are the Messiah of God. Help me to follow you!

Karla Manternach

Equal Opportunity Healing

Jesus said to the centurion, "You may go; as you have believed, let it be done for you." And at that very hour [his] servant was healed. Matthew 8:13

Let's face it. For many of us, one-to-one ministry comes most easily when we're helping people who are like us: our families or friends or neighbors. It's more difficult when we attempt to reach out to those who don't share our faith or political views or cultural background.

But there shouldn't be a difference. Jesus didn't turn away the centurion's plea for a paralyzed servant because the men were Gentiles. He healed Peter's mother-in-law even though her gender made her a second-class citizen.

There are qualities of Christ in all we serve: the young woman at an abortion clinic, the mentally ill and homeless man at the food pantry, the Latina who needs help fumigating her family's one-room apartment. When we fail to recognize that, we fail him.

Jesus, let me see you in everyone.

Melanie Rigney

Stepping Back

I say, then: live by the Spirit and you will certainly not gratify the desire of the flesh. Galatians 5:16

Moments of conversion seem to come when we least expect them. I was recently in the middle of a spirited conversation with my husband when I suddenly realized that my perception of the situation might not be correct. In fact, I became aware of my tendency to jump to the "only logical conclusion" without considering other explanations.

Self-righteousness can be a telltale sign that we are caught up in what Paul calls "the desire of the flesh." Nothing feeds our pride and inflames our rage like being convinced that we are on the right side of a cause. How many families and parishes have suffered permanent damage because no one was willing to step back and consider that their adversary's point of view might have some validity?

Spirit of love, continue to remind me that patience, kindness and generosity are the authentic signs of your presence.

Terri Mifek

AFRAID OF GOOD NEWS?

Immediately [Zechariah's] mouth was opened, his tongue freed, and he spoke blessing God. Then fear came upon all their neighbors, and all these matters were discussed throughout the hill country of Judea. Luke 1:64-65

So often in Scripture, fear seems to attach itself to good news: among the Bethlehem shepherds, the disciples at the Transfiguration and at the empty tomb on Easter morning. We seem to grow comfortable with ordinary life, even in its discouragements and apparent hopelessness. Give us a glimpse of something marvelous beyond expectation and we tremble.

Perhaps fear is somehow necessary, or at least predictable, when trying to deal with the extraordinary. But I don't want to get in the habit of expecting nothing from life so as to avoid disappointment. Some of Zechariah's and Elizabeth's neighbors probably decided that the whole story was bunk, and they logged another disappointment. But I think some took heart from the story of God's unexpected generosity and wondered what God would be up to next. I want to be like them.

Lord, help me believe good news when I hear it.

Mark Neilsen

MEASURING UP

Beware of false prophets, who come to you in sheep's clothing, but underneath are ravenous wolves. By their fruits you will know them. Do people pick grapes from thornbushes, or figs from thistles? Just so, every good tree bears good fruit, and a rotten tree bears bad fruit. Matthew 7:15-17

Prophets abounded during Jesus' time. So many people claimed to be sent by God that Jesus taught his followers to trust only those whose lives seemed to bear good fruit. Even today, a lot of people claim to be disciples of Christ. But what kind of people do they seem to be? Are they loving? Are they compassionate? Do they like people? Do they draw people to God and his Church, or do they drive people away? Are they arrogant and disdainful? Do they act as though only they are holy? At heart, this is a question of who among us truly seems to imitate Christ. That is our litmus test, for that is what it means to be a disciple. How about us? How do you and I measure up?

Jesus Christ, help me to be like you and to recognize you in others.

Karla Manternach

Savoring the Good

Taste and see how good the Lord is. Psalm 34:9

In a news story last summer, a man who had been experiencing health problems for two years finally learned that the source of his troubles was a plastic spoon lodged in his lung. Apparently he had eaten so quickly that he had swallowed the utensil without realizing what had happened. Granted, this is an extreme example, but if C. S. Lewis was right that "God shouts to us in our pain," our frantic pace might be taking a greater toll than we realize.

I am not contemplative by nature, so I often have to make a conscious choice to slow down and appreciate the gifts offered in the present moment. One way I do that is by focusing on one of my five senses. One day I pay special attention to what I see; on another I might notice scents or sounds. I have found that, even in the midst of difficult situations, this exercise leads to a deeper awareness of God's faithfulness as well as gratitude for all the good in my life.

Terri Mifek

Don't Miss Out

I did not come to call the righteous but sinners. Matthew 9:13

Jesus' encounters with the Pharisees never fail to entertain. Almost everywhere he preaches, a few of them show up, trying to compromise his ministry, to catch him in a violation of custom or law. Mingling with known sinners, as Jesus did repeatedly, was clearly unacceptable to the Pharisees.

While obeying the law is important—and Jesus was an observant Jew—he also knew the law and social strictures had their limitations. His message to the legalistic sticklers is straightforward, unadorned. He wants to engage real people on real issues, people with faults, problems, people searching for God. That means folks like you and me. And while he is not excluding the arrogantly self-righteous among us, he's pretty busy with the rest of humanity. His message is freely offered to any and all who will listen. If you're going to get hung up on the narrow applications of the law, you will be missing a life-changing message.

Paul Pennick

To Live More Kindly

Come and see the works of God... Psalm 66:5

What are the works of God? Do we recognize them? These works seem huge when written about in the Scriptures, but in our own lives, they are often passed over and unrecognized. Once in a while, these works startle us into attention. Such was the time when I learned of a woman whose car was damaged in a supermarket parking lot, crashed into by an undocumented immigrant. Upon learning he had no insurance, she decided not to press the issue, but someone else nearby called the police. The man was ticketed with a hefty fine. Instead of feeling self-righteous satisfaction, the woman went home and spoke with her husband. They decided to send what money they could to help pay the fine for the man. Such a small deed in the eyes of a large world, but how significant. When I heard of it, I felt I had experienced "the works of God." It inspired me to live more kindly.

Forgiving God, enlarge the love in my heart.

Sr. Joyce Rupp, O.S.M.

Acting Out of Love

You shall love the Lord, your God, with all your heart, with all your soul, and with all your mind. This is the greatest and the first commandment. The second is like it: You shall love your neighbor as yourself. Matthew 22:37-39

Let's consider for a moment what Jesus does not say. He does not say: Pray a great deal. Go to Mass on Sunday. Cultivate a simple lifestyle. Obey all the official teachings and rules and regulations of the Church. Read the Bible. Fast during Lent.

One hastens to say, of course, that any or all of these actions are good and reflect God's will for us; however, the point of Jesus' great commandment is that we must act out of total love for God and unconditional love for others. True discipleship, following Christ in today's world, means that everything we do we do out of love. Imagine that.

Lord Jesus, help me to act out of love in all things.

Mitch Finley

Who Is Jesus for Me?

Then he said to them, "But who do you say that I am?"

Luke 9:20

Jesus, I've too often avoided answering that question, pretending that it wasn't addressed to me. But today I want to at least try.

You are God, the holy and the awesome, the creator who is as different from me as light is from darkness. At least, that is how I want to be aware of you, even if I don't often acknowledge you as that kind of God.

You are a man, truly human, a real son of Mary, just as I am the son of my mother. That makes you, in some sense, just like me, just like every man and woman who ever lived and who ever will live. At least, that is how I want to know you, even if I often slip into the bad habit of denying your humanity. You are Messiah, my messiah, my savior, the one whose birth, life, death and resurrection made me eligible to be what I am—a child of God and an heir to eternal happiness. At least, that is who I want you to be for me, even if I don't act as if you are that savior.

You are friend and brother, my friend and my brother, the one who is always near me to console and to counsel, to comfort and to confront. At least, that is the friend and brother I want you to be.

James E. Adams

August 28

Help Me, Lord

> Jesus turned around and saw [the woman who touched his cloak], and said, "Courage, daughter! Your faith has saved you." And from that hour the woman was cured. Matthew 9:22

It's easy to go to God with problems when we already know the answers: Please show me how to be more patient. Help me to resist chocolate. Remind me how good I feel when I go to Mass.

But relying on heavenly guidance is harder in other situations: I don't understand why my friend had to die. I'm scared of growing old alone. I don't know what I'll do if I don't find a job soon.

At such times, being told to "turn it over to God" can sound pat and meaningless. But if we have the courage to acknowledge that, truly, God alone can help, that courage in the form of faith will save us. His help may not come in the form we expect or want, but it will come.

Lord, I ask for the courage and confidence to turn my afflictions over to you.

Melanie Rigney

Words as Gifts From God

You will be given at that moment what you are to say.

Matthew 10:19

A time of crisis can exact from the human heart words of truth that are nearly impossible to find—much less utter—in tranquil times. This is particularly true when the death of a loved one nears and words of deep, truthful love are spoken with tears and gratitude for the wondrous and fragile gift of human love.

There are other critical times as well. Deep hurt or resentment can and should be healed by the deeper currents of love. These currents may as well find words spoken in tears but rich in forgiveness. We all know the experience of waiting too long to speak what is deepest in our hearts. We ought to pray to use our time, our loves and our words wisely. All of these are gifts from God to us, and it is God who truly speaks through us when we love. Our best words are of him. Let us say a prayer that those words come in the ordinary times of life so that we can speak who we really are in him.

Fr. James Stephen Behrens, O.C.S.O.

Loving God and Neighbor

Teacher, what must I do to inherit eternal life? Luke 10:25

You might expect a lengthy answer for such an important question. But the answer Jesus gives is quite short. He simply tells you to love God with all the strength you have, and to love your neighbor as yourself. That's it! That's all you need! Love like that, and you will inherit eternal life.

Of course, it's easy to love when things go well, and we're surrounded by people we care about. But how do we love when things don't go well, and we're hurt by people who are selfish and insensitive? Perhaps that's the time to say to God, "Lord, I know what you are asking of me, but I find it hard to forgive. Please give me the strength to forgive as you do and to love as you love." We can trust in a favorable answer to this kind of prayer, for the compassionate Jesus has promised to be with us in all the difficulties of our lives.

Fr. Kenneth E. Grabner, C.S.C.

Following Jesus

Whoever does not take up his cross and follow after me is not worthy of me. Matthew 10:38

The spirituality I was taught growing up suggested practices in order to be worthy: penances and special prayers, reading and meditation, daily Mass and weekly confession, frequent visits to the Blessed Sacrament. These things were deeply graced, but they simply stopped being possible in my adult life. My time did not belong to me in the same way. It was filled with complex commitments, challenges and losses.

It took me a while to realize that these difficulties did not make me "unworthy," but that they were actually the cross I was to take up. Dealing with them with as much strength as I could muster, I was actually following after Jesus. I began to understand that these hard things had meaning, they had value, they were my part in the Paschal Mystery itself, serving in some way to help transform my life.

Jesus, help us to trust that we are following you as we take up the challenges of our complex lives.

Patricia Livingston

JUST GIVE IT AWAY

Cure the sick, raise the dead, cleanse lepers, drive out demons. Without cost you have received; without cost you are to give. Matthew 10:8

Like the apostles, we live in a quid-pro-quo society: You help me, and I'll help you. I can help you get a better job, lose weight or learn a new skill, but it'll cost you.

How radical, then, to be directed to help others simply because we can, with no expectation of a return on our investment. Yet that is precisely what Christ calls us to do: share our gifts without a thought for what we might receive spiritually, emotionally or financially. And the amazing thing is that when we act in Christ's name, we are repaid far more than we could have ever imagined—in love and faith and growth on our spiritual journeys.

Lord, help me to love the way you desire: unreservedly, with no expectation of reward.

Melanie Rigney

MERCIFUL SACRIFICE

**If you knew what this meant, "I desire mercy, not sacrifice,"
you would not have condemned these innocent men.**

Matthew 12:7

Jesus is referring to a passage from the prophet Hosea (6:6) in which God calls for a conversion of heart rather than mere outward displays of piety. This passage is sometimes cited to indicate that sacrifice, obedience and rules have no place in true religion. But Hosea is emphasizing God's preference for mercy and love over sacrifice, not insisting on a choice between them.

Obviously, sacrifice and love can go together as any good parent, loving spouse or faithful servant of the Church demonstrates all the time. But the fact is that sacrifice can also become loveless, pinched and full of resentment. When that happens, we will soon end up condemning anyone who does not observe the rules as meticulously as we think they should.

Neither worship of God nor love of neighbor can thrive without both mercy and sacrifice. With God's help, may we always keep them in the right order.

Mark Neilsen

SEPTEMBER 3

When the Word Takes Root

Hear then the parable of the sower. Matthew 13:18

The first thing Jesus does is admonish his disciples to "hear the parable." It's as if he says, "Look, I can explain this parable until I'm blue in the face, but it will do no good unless you listen to the parable first." So if you want understanding, go back and reread the parable itself, paying close attention to every word. Once we do that—maybe even two or three times—we can read the explanation of the parable that Jesus gives. Then we may realize that all of the examples Jesus gives apply to each one of us.

Sometimes I hear without understanding. Sometimes when I try to live the gospel, the minute I encounter some difficulty or opposition, I give up. Other times I allow "worldly anxiety" and financial worries to control my life. But it's also true that sometimes the word of God takes root in my life and bears fruit.

Lord Jesus, help me to admit that now and then I do it right.

Mitch Finley

Our Place of Refuge

There is no need for them to go away. Matthew 14:16

What a story—so good, it's told six times in the New Testament. A group of people comes together by chance or grace (Matthew's punch line: there were thousands that day). They're seekers, going out on foot from the cities to Jesus' secluded place. Not an easy trek.

Likely, they found more than they sought. If they were seeking silence and prayer, they found it. If they were seeking community, they found it. God's Word, healing, the real presence of God, a great, tender, personal love for each one: all these were there. Yet the disciples wanted to send them away to be fed. Where would they go? The food was among them. Once they'd found it, they didn't need to go away.

Where is our place of refuge? The place where we can simply stay and be fed in the presence of one another and our Beloved? What sort of trek would we make to get there?

Mary Marrocco

The Abundance of God

Whoever sows sparingly will also reap sparingly, and whoever sows bountifully will also reap bountifully. 2 Corinthians 9:6

Hard times. Some people hold on from paycheck to paycheck. Others scramble to survive without jobs. Many are grateful to be working at all. We get through hard times with stories. One story tells of making it on our own: To escape a wreck, each must fend for himself. Whatever we give away lessens our own chances. More common are the stories about support from friends, the kindness of strangers, faith in one's family, a responsive community.

Generosity gives us a glimpse of God. Like a shaft of light through a gray winter sky, the promise of abundance startles us. What is inexhaustible in a universe of vanishing resources? Even stars burn out eventually. In unexpected ways, hard times can awaken the heart. There is goodness that goes beyond balancing the books and the tough trade-offs of scarcity. The priceless is all around us. Reasons for gratitude crowd in the door that opens a crack.

Jeanne Schuler

Feeling at Home With Jesus

Live in love, as Christ loved us and handed himself over for us as a sacrificial offering to God for a fragrant aroma.

Ephesians 5:2

Even without a recession, selling a house can be difficult. I once heard that a realtor's trick was to have the seller bake bread the morning of an open house so the first thing a potential buyer would experience was the fresh bread aroma of a homey kitchen. Before any word is spoken, the fragrance itself makes the buyer more interested.

So, too, without an ounce of cologne, Jesus gave off a comforting warmth that welcomed people before he said a word, performed a healing or made a miraculous multiplication of food or drink. Jesus had an "air" about him, even a fragrance, that made people feel at home with him.

With Mother Teresa's words, we can pray:

Dear Jesus, help me to spread your fragrance everywhere that I go. Dear Jesus, flood my soul with your spirit and your love.

Fr. James Krings

The Preciousness of the Few

For where two or three are gathered together in my name, there am I in the midst of them. Matthew 18:20

We churchgoers are often impressed by numbers. We want to know how many people attended the fund-raiser or the parish mission. We get preoccupied with size: how big is our church, our school, our weekly collection? The problem comes when we equate numbers and size with effectiveness or worth. Such reckoning is directly contrary to the gospel.

Jesus underscored the value of one—for example, in the parable of the lost sheep. He also preached the preciousness of the few—as he does in this gospel verse. This means the small gathering in the tiny church in Podunk is just as precious as the large congregation in the huge cathedral in Big City.

If we looked at the world as Jesus does, we would appreciate things we might otherwise overlook or take for granted: a single lily, a lone sparrow, a baby's tiny fingernail, a small prayer group, one dear friend. Take time today to appreciate the single, the small, the few.

Jesus, help me to see the world through your eyes.

Sr. Melannie Svoboda, S.N.D.

Mercy Without End

Should you not have had pity on your fellow servant, as I had pity on you? Matthew 18:33

The love of money is a great disrupter of lives: loans not repaid, family squabbles over inheritance, spouses too discouraged to seek work, banks that stop lending. When money is missing, relationships often go sour. Jesus reminds us that spiritual life goes beyond the heart's resolve. The material conditions of our lives matter. Forgiveness brings debt relief. At times we are forgiven; at times we let go of old debts. Being forgiven frees us from failure so we can pass the gift of mercy on.

The master is harsh: The servant in debt is to be sold along with his family and belongings. Certainly we are more humane than these ancestors. In modern society, debtors go into bankruptcy, not off to prison. But the assurance of justice means little without mercy. How do we encounter those brought low by failure? Those in trouble often disappear behind walls that we drive past without a glance. When the cry for mercy goes unheard, no one is set free.

Jeanne Schuler

REVEALING THE KINGDOM

I give praise to you, Father...for although you have hidden these things from the wise and the learned you have revealed them to the childlike. Matthew 11:25

The wise and the learned, the scribes and the Pharisees, rejected Jesus' preaching and the significance of his mighty deeds. They did not recognize the presence of God among them. What is it in the childlike that disposes them to be receptive to the presence of God? Children have wonder in discovery. It contrasts with a "learned" sense that I already know what is important; I have already seen what there is to see.

On a plane recently, I was already into my book as we took off. A little voice in the row ahead cried, "Oh, wow! You can see the whole world up here!" She slipped from her seat belt and stood facing backwards, calling out to all of us behind her: "Look everybody, look! You can see the whole world up here!"

The whole world can be revealed to the childlike in us. We notice the wonder that the kingdom of God is right here before us.

Patricia Livingston

Treasures in Heaven

Again I say to you, it is easier for a camel to pass through the eye of a needle than for one who is rich to enter the kingdom of God. Matthew 19:24

Our culture is one of striving: We strive for more money, more things, more status, more everything. The cliché "more is more" pretty much sums us up. We know we can't take our bank account or our things with us when we leave this world, but it doesn't stop us from trying to amass more that our children and grandchildren will have to divide, distribute or dispose of. Scripture tells us to store our treasures in heaven, not down here. Maybe we need to spend more time thinking about the kinds of collections we want, the things of true value we can enjoy for all eternity.

My mother has always encouraged us to live lives of contentment. Instead of more is more, she maintains enough is enough. When we aren't clutching our things, we can embrace the real treasures. We can be rich in the ways that are pleasing to God.

Kristin Armstrong

KNOWING THE SHEPHERD

The LORD is my shepherd; I shall not want. Psalm 23:1

On a visit to rural Ireland, I saw a demonstration of sheepherding that stays with me still. A shepherd pressed into service one of his young border collies to help round up the flock of sheep scattered over the rolling hills.

The little collie's eyes blazed with excitement. Whether it was the shepherd's voice calling out directions for herding or the shepherd's whistled signals as the collie climbed out of his vocal range, the pup responded with single-minded intent. It seemed his one joy was to listen to the voice of the shepherd and follow his commands with wholehearted enthusiasm. To hear the shepherd's voice, to be in partnership with him, was clearly everything the dog needed.

I came away from that demonstration reflecting on my own relationship with the good Shepherd: When I listen to his voice, I have everything I need.

Loving God, thank you for shepherding me through each moment of my life.

Sr. Chris Koellhoffer, I.H.M.

Crosses and Opportunities

> We ourselves boast of you in the churches of God regarding your endurance and faith in all your persecutions and the afflictions you endure. 2 Thessalonians 1:4

One of the fundamental characteristics of authentic Christian faith is its tendency to see hard times, stressful situations and outright suffering of all kinds as both a cross and an opportunity. When we are afflicted, regardless of the cause, we pray for courage, patience and the grace to endure. But we also see such experiences as an opportunity to deepen our faith and trust in God, who invites us, nay insists, that we relate to him as our always-loving Father. No matter how dark our situation, no matter how afflicted we may be, no matter how hard the times we cannot avoid, our faith calls us to endure and to trust that our loving Father is involved here too, and hope is always appropriate.

Lord Jesus, help me to endure hard times and always be hopeful.

Mitch Finley

In Praise of Religious Women

Come here. I will show you the bride, the wife of the Lamb.

Revelation 21:9-10

This reading brings us right to the foot of the altar, where over the centuries hundreds of thousands of generous, humble and courageous women have responded to God's call to consecrated life through the profession of the evangelical counsels of poverty, chastity and obedience. The rich images of the Book of Revelation describe the Church both as a valiant woman arrayed in nuptial radiance and as a thriving metropolis, home to people from every corner of the earth. Throughout history, religious sisters have faithfully borne witness to both visions of the Church. As a spouse of Christ and welcoming refuge for all God's people, each religious woman expresses her deep love for God and God's people through her life of prayer and apostolic service, bearing daily witness to the gospel in the heart of the Church.

Have you ever met a religious sister? Even if your answer is no, without a doubt one is lifting you up to God at this very moment. Today, return the favor.

Claire J. King

Live Today

Therefore, stay awake! Matthew 24:42

Recently a young woman died suddenly of a ruptured aneurysm. It was sad, shocking and so unexpected. She was a vibrant person, and then she was gone.

Today Jesus reminds us all to "stay awake" because we "do not know on which day your Lord will come."

I do not think that Jesus is suggesting that we cower in fear. Rather, we are to live life with courage and faith, and live it to the fullest. We are to live as if each day is our last. One day it will be.

And if we do, when the Master comes, we will be ready.

Msgr. Stephen J. Rossetti

Finding True Wisdom

For the wisdom of this world is foolishness in the eyes of God... 1 Corinthians 3:19

I have several friends and colleagues at work whom I consider to be truly wise. They are intelligent, well-educated, thoughtful, sensitive, have common sense and always seem to know exactly the right words to say. My life would be poorer without them.

And then there's God. I don't always understand him, and the wisdom of his word is often looked down on by those who don't know him at all. My God is often the butt of jokes. The teachings of God often go against what is called "conventional wisdom." His commandments ask me to do things my friends would never ask of me. And yet, my life would be incomprehensible without my God.

God, thank you for the wise people in my life. But never allow my faith in that wisdom to overshadow the true knowledge that comes from you alone.

Steve Givens

Embracing Change

No one who has been drinking old wine desires new, for he says, "The old is good." Luke 5:39

Jesus uses the metaphor of new wine and old wineskins after a discussion with the disciples. They wonder why he does not have them fast when John the Baptist insists that his followers fast. Jesus stretches the disciples to move beyond their current spiritual practice. He's not saying fasting is never valuable. Rather, he is telling them that fasting is not what is presently needed.

Change is difficult for most of us. Who wants to let go of what feels comfortable and has been "the right thing" to do? Yet we won't mature spiritually unless we are willing to let go and enter a period of new growth. When I am resisting strongly, it's usually an indication that I should ease up on my tight grip and open up to new possibilities.

Sr. Joyce Rupp, O.S.M.

When a Relationship Is Harmful

Do you not know that a little yeast leavens all the dough?

1 Corinthians 5:6

My first real job was working for a nonprofit organization I greatly admired. I worked hard there and enjoyed it. Then I became friends with a coworker who did not think much of our employer. At the time, I thought my friend had special insight into the organization—that he saw things I didn't. Looking back, I think he was just jaded. All the same, I joined him in gossip and nit-picking. My work morale plummeted.

Sometimes a relationship can be toxic. Like yeast activating a dough, it only takes a small measure of negativity or dysfunction to infiltrate our whole lives. This can keep us from living as God calls us to live. It can keep us from loving others as we ought. Is there a destructive relationship in your life? Does it stand between you and being faithful to the gospel? Should you limit the time you spend with that person? How else might God expect you to relate differently to each other?

God, help me to be faithful to you in all my relationships.

Karla Manternach

Out in Public

> **I announced your justice in the vast assembly;**
> **I did not restrain my lips, as you, O Lord, know.** Psalm 40:10

In working for more than 15 years in Catholic television, I've "announced" God's justice hundreds of times. Covering countless stories, I presented the Church's position on numerous topics. While television is a very public ministry, I was largely working in a "safe" environment—dealing with other Catholics who were active in their faith and proud to be so.

Relating the faith in real time to the general public is very different. I admit that I have hesitated to bless myself when eating out. I marvel at those who unabashedly walk through the streets participating in a eucharistic procession or in a live Way of the Cross.

So many people are desperately searching for answers to the fundamental questions of life. The "vast assembly" is hurting because they are seeking solutions in worldly things. Our faith has the answers. In some manner today, can we provide just a small public reminder that Jesus can heal their hurts?

Terence Hegarty

THE CALL TO DISCIPLESHIP

When day came, he called his disciples to himself, and from them he chose Twelve, whom he also named apostles.

Luke 6:13

After Jesus spent a night in prayer on the mountain, he chose the twelve apostles. Did he walk through the crowd and tap certain ones on the shoulder? Maybe he stood outside the group and called out twelve names. Were they surprised—thinking perhaps they were unqualified for this new and unexpected position? Jesus has told us that all his followers are called in some way to minister to others. Gifts and talents are given to be shared in order to promote the kingdom of God on earth.

I always find it puzzling how God calls people to various positions. When I think about my call to priesthood, I don't have a clear answer. I did not hear God speak my name or feel a hand on my shoulder. I must have heard a call when I was spending some nighttime prayer with Jesus on the mountain.

Lead me, Lord, to life's fulfillment.

Fr. James McKarns

READ, PRAY, ACT

We will buy the lowly man for silver, and the poor man for a pair of sandals. Amos 8:6

This reading from Amos is not hard to understand. Wealthy and powerful people are exploiting the poor and the weak, and God is not pleased.

Connecting this text with our own world is not so hard either. There are many exploited workers today. Without a too-young teen in a factory in Thailand and an undocumented immigrant in a slaughterhouse in Georgia, my running shoes and tonight's chicken dinner would have cost me a little more.

But there is a danger in this easy text—the danger of merely bemoaning: "Isn't it terrible the way workers are sometimes treated?" "Isn't it terrible the way I comfortably benefit from it?" Moral indignation is no substitute for action, and blanket self-condemnation is actually an obstacle to action. And it is action that Amos' words are intended to inspire.

What should I do, alone or with others, to help bring aid to someone who is suffering economic injustice? God is not commanding us to change the world but to take a constructive step, even a small one.

Kevin Perrotta

SEPTEMBER 21

FALL'S BEAUTY AND PREDICTABILITY

**Teach us to number our days aright,
that we may gain wisdom of heart.** Psalm 90:12

Where I live in northeast Ohio, September is when the fall foliage is in its full glory. Everywhere I look I behold trees of bright red, orange, yellow and even gold. It's a sight that amazes me every year, one I never take for granted. As I watch the leaves falling, I find myself saying, "What a way to go! In such splendor!"

The beauty and predictability of fall helps me believe in the goodness and constancy of God. Fall comes. Summer is over. Winter is on its way. And even though fall appears to be a season of death, it isn't really. The trees are not dying. Their precious vitality is stored in their intricate root systems beneath the ground. When outward circumstances change (and they will), these same trees will sprout brand new green leaves. Fall is a sign of the ingenuity of God. When things appear to be dead, new life bursts forth.

Source of All Wisdom, help me to see possibilities where I am tempted to see only death.

Sr. Melannie Svoboda, S.N.D.

Appreciating Solitude

Once when Jesus was praying in solitude, and the disciples were with him... Luke 9:18

We think of solitude as time spent alone in a place devoid of noise, but on this occasion, Jesus is described as praying in solitude even though he is accompanied by his disciples.

This seems to be a contradiction, but I recall an experience I had years ago while on an extended silent retreat. I had spent much of the time alone grieving the recent death of my mother, but on the final day, I decided to walk into the nearby town and found myself drawn to the swings on a bustling playground on a busy street. Although I was surrounded by commotion as I began to swing, I was overwhelmed by a joyful and intimate connection with God.

Interior quiet is more a disposition of the heart than the absence of external noise. The more we make a practice of spending time apart from the hustle and bustle, the more readily we will be aware of God's indwelling presence, no matter where we are.

Terri Mifek

September 23

Urgency in Following Christ

I will follow you wherever you go. Luke 9:57

Two words come to mind in reflecting on this gospel: "urgency" and "sacrifice." Jesus is saying: Following me is so urgent that it allows no delay, and it calls for sacrifice. Yes, he's using hyperbole, but he's trying to make us think. He usually had a place to stay, but he couldn't always count on it. Neither can the disciples always expect to be welcomed and appreciated. Burying one's parent is a serious religious duty; so is maintaining family ties. But being a disciple and proclaiming the gospel is even more important.

We are called today to renew our commitment to follow Christ along that journey—and embrace the urgency and sacrifice that go with it. But don't forget the other side: the good news. When we accept the urgency and sacrifice, then we discover the satisfactions, the deep joys of being a disciple that far outweigh the burdens. No product can give a warranty like that. And that is why Christianity has not died out.

Lord Jesus, renew my commitment to be your faithful disciple, no matter the cost.

Fr. Martin Pable, O.F.M. Cap.

GROWING IN FAITH

As we have said before, and now I say again, if anyone preaches to you a gospel other than the one that you received, let that one be accursed! Galatians 1:9

St. Paul was trying to keep the community of new believers in the Roman province of Galatia faithful to God the Father through Jesus Christ, but it may well have been that their harder challenge was yet to come. Maturing in faith requires Christians to embody the gospel—to grow in and with it into ever fuller and dynamic commitment.

How hard and how freeing it is to take responsibility to enflesh the gospel of Jesus today, to allow the Living Word to speak intimately in the silence of our hearts and to bear witness to that Word through our actions in the world.

Lord Jesus, help us to grow daily with the precious gospel we first received.

Claire J. King

SEPTEMBER 25

Teaching Others to Pray

Lord, teach us to pray... Luke 11:1

The image of a child kneeling at bedside praying while a parent watches can seem like an idyllic scene from the past. Similar images, such as a family around the dinner table with heads bowed in prayer, can also appear as a nostalgic painting from a bygone era.

Jesus taught his disciples to pray. He gave them, and us, a prayer that has been recited down through the ages. Jesus spent much time in prayer and helped his disciples do the same.

Praying and teaching others to pray is an essential part of spiritual parenthood, then and now. Perhaps, as generations pass, some forms of prayer will change. But the words of Jesus, passed down from parent to child, will always remain: "Father, hallowed be your name..."

Have you ever helped someone to pray?

Msgr. Stephen J. Rossetti

Because We Sin, We Need Saving

This saying is trustworthy and deserves full acceptance:
Christ Jesus came into the world to save sinners.

1 Timothy 1:15

People can often admit they have failed, made a mistake, were weak, exercised poor judgment—there are many other synonyms—but we seldom hear someone say he or she has sinned. Why are we so reluctant to admit we have sinned?

I would like to declare here and now, I have sinned, and, therefore, I am a sinner. I need to admit this because Jesus came into the world to save sinners. If I refuse to acknowledge I am a sinner, how can I get enrolled in his saving plan? If I am not a sinner, then I don't need a savior. That is much too risky. I know I am in need of a savior. I need grace, guidance, forgiveness and inspiration to be a follower of the one who saves sinners. Being a sinner does not mean I am a gangster, mobster, desperado or terrorist. It means I've broken spiritual laws and I need the mercy and forgiveness of my Savior.

Jesus, don't forget I'm a sinner. Thanks for being our Savior. I am most grateful!

Fr. James McKarns

September 27

GIVING OURSELVES AWAY

"Go, sell what you have, and give to [the] poor...then come, follow me." At that statement his face fell, and he went away sad, for he had many possessions. Mark 10:21-22

What a poignant reversal in this man's encounter with Jesus! His humble goodness is so touching that Jesus "looking at him, loved him." But faced with selling all he has, he goes away sad. Other translations of this incident call it the story of the rich, young man. I like to think his sadness was not the end of the story, but that, as often happens, life itself gave him other opportunities to give what he had to the poor.

For most of us, great wealth is not what we have to give. But, often in some kind of crisis, we are asked to give up our time, privacy, peace of mind, sense of ourselves as in charge of our lives, to care for someone in need. We are asked to give ourselves away, following Jesus.

Jesus, as I struggle with what life asks me to give away, let me know that you look on me, love me.

Patricia Livingston

Our Images of Jesus

There is a baptism with which I must be baptized, and how great is my anguish until it is accomplished! Luke 12:50

We walk around with an understanding of Jesus in our heads. We hear his name or we turn to him in prayer, and we do so, often unconsciously, with a preconceived notion of him in our hearts. What is your preconceived notion of Jesus? Is he gentle and non-judgmental? Strong? Understanding and forgiving? How has your image of Jesus been shaped by artistic portrayals?

One lesson we may learn from this reading is that regardless of how serene Jesus may have been at times, there were also times when he was anything but serene. Today, Jesus refers to his "anguish," describing it as "great." We do well to ponder the great anguish of Jesus when we examine our images of him. For starters, we can realize that this means the risen Lord understands our anguish; he knows what it feels like. Give it some thought.

Lord Jesus, be with me when I know anguish, and help me to rely on you.

Mitch Finley

Learning to Love

Husbands, love your wives… [Wives,] respect [your] husband.
Ephesians 5:25, 33

Any married person knows that loving and respecting your spouse is not always easy. We don't always feel loving or loved, lovable or worthy of respect. Relationship is difficult because we ourselves are such a mix of beauty and goodness on the one hand, selfishness and sinfulness on the other.

Learning how to give and receive love and respect is one of the delights and challenges of marriage—and of human life in general. Married or not, it's our Christian duty and joy to become loving and loved. But we must work this out here on earth, amidst conflict and pain and temptation, falling and getting up again, asking and giving forgiveness along the way. It would be impossible if we were trying to create love. It's possible because Love created us. Throughout our lives, it woos and shapes us. As St. Paul tells us, loving this way means becoming like Christ.

Thank you, Lord, for trusting that we can learn to love as you do.

Mary Marrocco

Overcoming Fear

Praised be the L ORD, I exclaim,
and I am safe from my enemies. Psalm 18:4

As a young child, I was so shy that I would pray that the teacher wouldn't call on me even when I knew the answer. Over time, my anxiety grew, and I began to avoid any situation that might require me to do any type of public speaking. Fear was definitely my enemy, one which seemed destined to defeat me.

Then one day I began to pray to be liberated from this crippling fear. The answer to my prayer came quickly when I was asked and agreed to do a reading at Mass. My initial leap of faith led to many more small steps over the years until this particular fear has disappeared.

While we might have people in our lives that we consider adversaries, our greatest enemies are often those that reside in our hearts and minds. How and when healing takes place remains a mystery, but the first step is to ask.

Terri Mifek

The Astounding Faith of Job

**The Lord gave and the Lord has taken away;
blessed be the name of the Lord!** Job 1:21

This declaration from Job surely ranks as one of the greatest professions of faith in the Bible. It is all the more astounding because it came in a period when conventional wisdom held that the loss of material possessions was a sure sign of God's disfavor. To "bless" God in the face of personal disaster was equivalent to Job praising God even as Job felt he was being cast into hell!

To be filled with praise when "God gives" is easy for most of us. We come to expect health, welfare and happiness. We are grateful for those, although most of us don't thank God often enough.

But to be filled with praise when "God takes away" is very difficult for us. When disaster strikes, our faith is very often too weak to continue seeing God as benevolent. We are tempted to say, "There is no God" or "God doesn't care."

When disaster strikes, pray for the gift of the faith of Job, who held fast to the belief that what God wanted for him was good even if he couldn't understand it.

James E. Adams

A Gracious Presence to All

> They are to slander no one, to be peaceable, considerate, exercising all graciousness toward everyone. Titus 3:2

In Paul's letter to Titus, he lists some of the duties for Christians living on the island of Crete. These duties apply to us today too. If we could fully engage in these responsibilities, what a difference it would make. In order to be more attentive to these prescribed duties, we might begin by trying to activate one of them each day.

On Sunday we would do our best to avoid speaking or thinking unkindly about anyone. The next day we would live as peacefully as possible, avoiding arguments, irritable comments and the need to be right. On Tuesday we would have the challenge of being caring and considerate to everyone (no exceptions), and the rest of the week we would make every effort to be a gracious presence no matter what the situation happened to be. If we managed to do that, we could well have a truly spirit-transforming week.

Jesus, help me live in a way that reflects your teachings.

Sr. Joyce Rupp, O.S.M.

DON'T LOOK BACK

Whoever seeks to preserve his life will lose it, but whoever loses it will save it. Luke 17:33

When we try too hard to win, we lose. When we try too hard to please, we disappoint. When we try too hard to be liked, we are disliked. When we put ourselves first, we end up last. When we seek our own glory, we stumble. God must love irony.

When God pries open our tight grip on the things we cling to, we find so much more as we finally agree to let go.

When we value this life and the things of this world over the things of eternity, we miss the entire point. We value fleeting over forever, dust over destiny.

Jesus is telling us to submit. Submit our daily lives now, and submit our future when our day comes. Let's keep a loose grip on this world, so when it's time to go, we don't look back. No regrets.

Kristin Armstrong

Singing to God

O God, I will sing a new song to you. Psalm 144:9

"Guess what, Sister?" my fifth-grader Estelle blurted out. "Sometimes my heart's words become a song to God. That's called prayer." It was a fitting reminder that God loves to hear the lyrics in our hearts even if, like that November day, I was singing the spiritual blues.

In the psalmist's hymn today, we chant a promise: We will sing a new song. The "new" depends on what we need God to do for us. Perhaps we hope God showers us with amazing grace; comforts us by trading our life's rugged cross for a crown; transforms us into channels of peace; unites us more deeply as one bread, one body. In singing each day from our heart, our prayer will be sincere and will bellow forth in expectation and praise to our God from whom all blessings flow.

Sr. Bridget Haase, O.S.U.

October 5

Clinging to Our Treasure

> You are lacking in one thing. Go, sell what you have, and give to [the] poor and you will have treasure in heaven; then come, follow me. Mark 10:21

How wonderful to receive an invitation like this! But the man Jesus invited was rich, and his wealth prevented him from doing what Jesus asked. This gospel story prompts us to ask if there is something that keeps us from following Jesus. Perhaps Jesus asks us to let go of our anger or our fear or our selfishness. These are all things that would keep us from following him with free and loving minds and hearts.

The rich man refused Jesus' invitation and so lost the chance to change his life. Of course, it would have been hard for him to give up his wealth, just as it may be hard for us to give up our particular attachments. But Jesus tells us in this gospel that what is impossible for us is possible for God.

Lord, I trust in your power to help me follow you as you will.

Fr. Kenneth E. Grabner, C.S.C.

A Living Truth

> **But you have the anointing that comes from the holy one, and you all have knowledge.** 1 John 2:20

This beautiful little passage from the first letter of John can serve as a call to totally embrace Christ. Be absorbed in Christ. Put any kind of denial far away. We have probably all experienced anti-Christ moments in our lives. This does not mean we have outright denied Christ, but we can profess to be a Christian and be quite irresponsible in living the law of Christ. If you have difficulty with the concept of law, try looking at it as a little light that guides you on the way, leading you to truth.

In this text, we are given a lovely affirmation to help us lean toward faithfulness and truth. The author reminds us that we have knowledge. Furthermore, we possess an anointing that comes from the holy one.

Christ, your words help me in my longing for the truth. May the anointing I have received from you remain deep in the recesses of my life that I may never be a living lie but rather a living truth.

Sr. Macrina Wiederkehr, O.S.B.

Laying Aside Our Prejudices

But Nathanael said to him, "Can anything good come from Nazareth?" Philip said to him, "Come and see." John 1:46

Nathanael was prejudiced. He couldn't believe that anyone of any worth could come from a hick town like Nazareth. Yet he was able to lay aside his prejudice—at least temporarily—and follow Philip to see this Jesus for himself. And when he met Jesus, he was so swept off his feet by him that he became a disciple.

We all have our prejudices. Perhaps we look down on people of a certain age. Or maybe we're turned off by purple hair, tattoos or three-piece suits. Or maybe we're too quick to label individuals as radical, conservative, strange, lazy, dishonest or no good. Wisdom comes when we are able to identify our prejudices and, laying them aside, "go and see" for ourselves.

Jesus, give me the eyes to see goodness in everyone.

Sr. Melannie Svoboda, S.N.D.

FAITHFUL—MOMENT TO MOMENT

Take care, brothers, that none of you may have an evil and unfaithful heart, so as to forsake the living God. Encourage yourselves daily while it is still "today," so that none of you may grow hardened by the deceit of sin. Hebrews 3:12-13

This passage urges us to "live in the now"—a trendy idea, and also an ancient one. It calls us to open our hearts to God, be faithful to him and guard against evil. We are to choose God every day, watching out for the hardness that comes from thinking I can forgive later, when I'm good and ready. I can do the right thing later, when I have more time. I can help my neighbors later, because they will still be there.

Discipleship is a lifelong endeavor, but it is lived out one choice at a time. Our fidelity to God takes place moment to moment, day to day. It expresses itself in our decisions, large and small, and in doing the right thing now while we still have the chance.

Gracious God, help me be faithful while it is still today.

Karla Manternach

OCTOBER 9

Keep Holy the Sabbath

The sabbath was made for man, not man for the sabbath.

Mark 2:27

This quote is often offered as proof that Jesus had no interest in religious rules. Man, that is, human beings, do not exist simply to fulfill their Sunday obligations. Fair enough, but what about the first part of Jesus' statement? Why was the sabbath made for us in the first place?

The sabbath traditionally gives us not only rest from the routines of work, but also, and more importantly, reminds us who we are in relationship to God. The requirement that Catholics attend Mass on Sunday, for example, keeps us grounded in our deepest beliefs.

I owe God this worship as a matter of justice, but God has no needs at all. Filled with more needs than I care to count, I am the one who benefits from the sabbath observance—or who suffers from my failures to take it seriously. And like any good parent, God is pleased to see me eat well, get enough sleep and show up on Sunday morning.

Lord, help me to keep Sundays holy.

Mark Neilsen

Drinking From Jesus' Cup

You do not know what you are asking. Can you drink the cup that I drink…? Mark 10:38

What an endearingly human picture is painted of James and John here! Endearing? You may be inclined to smirk at their self-centered request. Before judging them too harshly for their desire to have first place in the reign of God, remember that these are two of the disciples Jesus chose to take with him to the Mount of Transfiguration. Even when we are specially chosen by Jesus, we are capable of having grandiose dreams that don't quite fit our vocation.

We are called to serve. We are also called to drink of the cup from which Jesus drinks. It is a cup of darkness, a cup of suffering. In my experience, this cup of suffering usually holds a hidden gift, an obscure grace. We may have to hold the cup longer than we wish to discover the gift. Seldom is the gift visible as we drink.

Help me trust even the darkness, that I may never turn away from the invisible gift.

Sr. Macrina Wiederkehr, O.S.B.

AN ACT OF FAITH

Grieved at their hardness of heart, he said to the man, "Stretch out your hand." Mark 3:5

A friend who says he is an atheist once challenged me: "Prove to me that God answers prayers, and I'll consider believing." Yet I knew he would explain away any attempt I would make, especially any stories of miracles. Miracles, he had previously told me, do not and cannot happen, for they go against the laws of reason and science. So he asked for proof but didn't really want it and wasn't prepared to accept it. As sure as I am of God's ability to reach into our lives and act, I was speechless.

Perhaps a better response would have been to ask a question: "When was the last time you tried reaching out to God?" Like Peter taking that first step out of the boat on his miraculous walk across the water, God's miracles often follow when we fist make our own faltering small act of faith—when we step out of the boat or stretch out our hands, expecting to be healed.

Jesus, see me, reaching out to you.

Steve Givens

A PRAYER SET TO MUSIC

**He put a new song into my mouth,
a hymn to our God.** Psalm 40:4

When I was a child, I did not sing at Mass. I just listened to the choir. Since the Second Vatican Council, the Church has encouraged the whole congregation to sing. We come to the eucharistic liturgy for participation, not just observation. Someone humorously said, "If we sing well, we encourage others to sing. If we don't sing well, we encourage others to sing—so they don't hear us."

The key factor is that the Lord hears us even if we are off-key. Our modern liturgical songs give us many beautiful teachings. I have been impressed by the workshops I have attended, conducted by some of our well-known musicians. They have spent numerous hours coordinating correct theology with colorful words and the flow of pleasant music. Singing a religious song is offering a prayer to God. I believe if it takes a little more effort to sing my prayer, the Lord may be even more pleased with my prayer.

Lord Jesus, I'm planning to sing a new song to you.

Fr. James McKarns

Helping Us Hear

Whoever has ears to hear ought to hear. Mark 4:9

Why is it so hard to hear God's Word?

Here, as they often do, the disciples can be of help to us. Jesus was talking to a crowd so large he had to speak from a boat on the sea. He told them a parable. Mark's Gospel doesn't tell us whether any of the people were able to hear, but he does say the disciples, Jesus' special followers including the Twelve, had trouble hearing. Thank goodness—even though we struggle to hear God's Word, we can still belong to Christ.

To help them hear, Jesus gave the disciples a special explanation. We, too, can get special explanations, through homilies and spiritual reading, talking to each other, Bible study and the like. We need to do this work, but on its own, it won't get us there. What will get us there, Jesus says, is this: We've been given the mystery of the kingdom. The more we allow the mystery to dwell in us, the stronger our ears will grow.

Thank you, Lord, for ears that hear, for a heart that receives your mystery.

Mary Marrocco

Heal Me, Jesus...Later

Then they began to beg [Jesus] to leave their district.

Mark 5:17

Jesus is traveling through the Gentile territory of the Gerasenes when he comes upon a possessed man whose misery is described in vivid detail. Jesus relieves this man of his suffering by sending his demons into a nearby herd of 2,000 swine. The swine then race down into the sea and drown. When the people of the town come to see what has happened, their reaction is most curious: They beg Jesus to leave.

Why didn't they embrace Jesus instead of sending him away? Perhaps they couldn't afford to lose more swine. What would we do if some itinerant holy man sent demons into our computers? Or maybe these folks were aware of their lesser demons and didn't want to deal with someone so powerful as Jesus. If we have some "demon" addiction, temper, laziness, unwholesome lifestyle to which we aren't quite ready to bid farewell, are we tempted to beg Jesus to leave?

Lord Jesus, with your grace, I welcome you and beg you never to leave.

Paige Byrne Shortal

October 15

The Need for Solitude

Come away by yourselves to a deserted place and rest a while. Mark 6:31

Henri Nouwen wisely noted, "Somewhere we know that without a lonely place, our lives are in danger." Jesus and Nouwen were not referring to loneliness. They were urging a temporary departure from others in order to have the essential quiet space for a healthy inner life. Jesus' invitation came out of his experience of being immersed in constant activity. People hungered for his presence and healing abilities. He knew the importance of going apart for prayer and renewal. Every person needs some solitude. Parents with young children long for even snippets of it. So do people forced to work two or three jobs to pay their bills. Monks and nuns would seem to have a sufficient amount of solitude, but even they must make real efforts to attain enough of it. Today, rather than bemoaning the inhumane tendency of people being busy every moment of their waking hours, it is more valuable to set an example by deliberately taking time for our own necessary solitude.

Sr. Joyce Rupp, O.S.M.

Holy, Holy, Holy!

Holy, holy, holy is the Lord of hosts! …All the earth is filled with his glory! Isaiah 6:3

Finding these words in Isaiah stuns me. We still say them at every eucharistic liturgy! Isaiah's call—which follows in this chapter—happened in 742 B.C. Almost 3,000 years later, we praise God with these words, which scholars say may have been from the liturgy of the Jerusalem Temple. God's holiness manifests as glory seen through all the earth. In Christian revelation, the glory, the power and presence of God are revealed as love.

Something stirs us to this prayer when we see the glory of love. At a recent family event, there was a cousin from Argentina, a tiny ten-year-old, terribly shy. My granddaughter Trish noticed the girl clinging to her father's hand by the door. She skipped over and, knowing a little Spanish, just pointed to a plate of cupcakes on a side table, motioned her to come pick one, then took her to a seat near a puppy to eat. At the end of the evening, they gave each other a hug. Watching, I said to God, "Holy, holy, holy."

Patricia Livingston

October 17

Embracing the Fullness of Life

For freedom Christ set us free; so stand firm and do not submit again to the yoke of slavery. Galatians 5:1

Various forms of slavery bind us all. Some of us struggle under the slavery of a bad temper; for others it is the slavery of past wounds or the slavery of the ego. At times it can feel like there is no way out of our slavery, that we are destined to be forever chained in captivity. But taking a step back and viewing our situation from a different perspective can sometimes help. I often struggle with the slavery of "the should"—that inner voice that declares, "I should do this." It is so easy for me to be pulled into this form of slavery and allow it to guide my decisions. Some decisions, unfortunately, continue to play out for years, or even decades. Over time I have learned that my slavery to "the should" is rooted in my fears and insecurities. This awareness has helped me make some better decisions. God does not want us enslaved by our insecurities and fears—God desires us to be free.

God of freedom, help us cast off the yoke of slavery and embrace the fullness of life that you offer everyone.

David Nantais

Jesus, Not Ignorance, Is Bliss

> The God of Abraham, the God of Isaac, and the God of Jacob, the God of our fathers, has glorified his servant Jesus...
>
> Acts 3:13

The people in Jesus' time were amazed by the healings that were occurring around them. They attributed the miraculous works to Peter and John, not recognizing that the healing power came from Jesus. "You acted out of ignorance," they are told.

As Christians, we cannot claim such ignorance. We know much more about Jesus and his divine nature.

But before we feel superior to the contemporaries of the apostles, we could ask ourselves how often we have failed to recognize Jesus in others. Every day, in both dramatic and seemingly mundane fashion, miracles still occur, souls are still saved. Through Christ may we understand that we serve as modern-day apostles, bringing this knowledge of who Jesus really is to all those whom we encounter.

Jesus, my Savior, help me listen to you; fill my mind and heart with your knowledge and peace.

Terence Hegarty

October 19

Don't Settle
for 'Not Bad'

The last condition of that person is worse than the first.

Luke 11:26

When I'm with little children in a store full of breakables, I tell them it's a "hands-behind-the-back" store. As they clasp their little hands behind their backs, they are less tempted to touch as they wander through the aisles. Sometimes it's easier and more effective to do something than to refrain from doing something else.

Jesus explains that when a bad spirit is exorcised, if a good spirit doesn't take its place, that bad spirit will return with its bad-spirit friends and the person will be worse off than before. It is the same with bad habits. To rid oneself of a bad habit, it is best to form a new habit. Instead of time in front of a computer or TV screen, take a walk. Instead of gossip, praise someone. Instead of overindulging, give to others. Instead of complaining, give thanks. It is not enough to be "not bad." We are created for the good.

Paige Byrne Shortal

RISE UP!

Jesus said to him, "Rise, take up your mat, and walk."

John 5:8

This man was ill, blind, lame and crippled. I have felt degrees of all of these things in my times of brokenness. My sin has made me sick. I have not been able to see myself or my situation clearly. I have been stuck, unable to move forward. I have been broken and betrayed, flat on my mat.

Jesus came to me in that sad state. He speaks words of peace and power. He has compassion for our mess and our pain. But praise God, our Savior does not leave us mired in it. Rise, he says. Get off that mat. Pick it up and walk. I hear his voice clearly. Shake off that self-pity and rise up. He does his part, the healing. We do our part, the walking.

Do you feel flat on your mat today? Jesus is calling us to dust off and move on.

Kristin Armstrong

VINDICATION FOR THE JUST

If the just one be the son of God, he will defend him and deliver him from the hand of his foes. Wisdom 2:18

Isn't this what we all want to believe: that if a person is doing what God wants, he or she will be protected from harm, especially from the wickedness of other people? But our experience tells us that isn't so. And it wasn't so for Jesus himself.

The thinking expressed in this passage from the Book of Wisdom reflects a misunderstanding of what it means for God to care for us. Those who think this way know "not the hidden counsels of God" (verse 22). From the perspective of this brief life on earth, the just one's fate seems tragic, even pointless. But viewed from the eternal love of God, there is reward and vindication for the righteous.

That is our hope, a hope that is beyond the schemes and calculations of worldly wisdom.

Lord Jesus, strengthen my faith in your eternal care for me and those I love.

Mark Neilsen

Walking Together

Neither do I condemn you. John 8:11

How sweetly, simply these words fall from the lips of Jesus. Often we're braced to hear the opposite from God. Perhaps that's what keeps us from approaching him at times. At other times, like the would-be stoners of the adulterous woman in this gospel, we might be expecting him to judge others—those we've already judged and found unworthy—and taken aback when he doesn't.

The 23rd Psalm promises quiet waters, comfort and guidance, a table laden and a cup overflowing unconditionally—not because we never fail, but because his love never fails.

When he extends mercy, can we receive it as it flows freely to us all? Can we walk together by those waters?

Merciful one, open me to the goodness and loving kindness that infuse my life, and let me become a bearer of your peace.

Mary Marrocco

October 23

JOY: A TRUE SIGN OF GOD

Thus Philip went down to the city of Samaria and proclaimed the Christ to them… There was great joy in that city. Acts 8:5, 8

In the Acts of the Apostles and the letters of Paul, the response of people who began to believe was joy. It reminds me of Leon Bloy's line: "Joy is the most infallible sign of the presence of God." What a treasure to cherish!

But I find that joy can be overwhelmed. Just as a migraine can ruin a picnic, painful happenings can eclipse joy. In a hard time recently, I remembered a friend's grandmother showing me her "joy safe," a wooden box in which she kept things that connected her with joy and reminded her of God's presence. I started my own box with two things: a button from the uniform my father wore when he came safely home from war and a note from a grandchild who had been kept back in third grade: "Grandma! I got all As. I'm gonna make it."

Dear God, thank you for joy—help us keep it safe.

Patricia Livingston

Which God Will We Serve?

We will not serve your god or worship the golden statue...

Daniel 3:18

When the word got out that Daniel and his friends refused to bow down, the king threatened them with death. When they remained steadfast, he ordered them to be cast into a fiery furnace. To the king's dismay, the flames did not harm them. This convinced him he'd better not mess with these fellows, and he set them free.

I think of this story when I watch TV ads for cars or other products that appear almost godlike. Or when screaming fans throw themselves at the latest rock stars. But the truth is: All of us are tempted to place something or someone else in place of the true God. It is often something good: our career, our hobby, a favorite sport, a person we love and admire. It is often said that the First Commandment is the hardest of all to observe: "I am the Lord... you shall not place other gods above me." Today is a good time to examine ourselves: Who—or what—is the god I am serving?

Fr. Martin Pable, O.F.M. Cap.

Loving Extravagantly

The house was filled with the fragrance of the oil. John 12:3

Many of us, through choice or economic necessity, have had to learn to live frugally. We try to practice making careful, deliberate choices, conscious of their effect on both our own household budget and the implications for the larger world.

So, of course, we take notice and stand in awe of the contrast we see in Mary's grand gesture: anointing Jesus with a liter of perfume that must have blown nearly a year's income. Like the lives of the holy ones given over in love and service without calculation of the cost, Mary's dramatic act of extravagance filled the entire home, enveloping all those present and lingering on in memory. More, her seemingly wasteful act profoundly comforted a dear friend who at that very moment was courageously inching closer to the longest, most tortuous journey of his life.

Even today, the fragrance of such a gesture remains among us.

Sr. Chris Koellhoffer, I.H.M.

Spending Ourselves for God

Though I thought I had toiled in vain,
   and for nothing, uselessly, spent my strength,
Yet my reward is with the Lord… Isaiah 49:4

During the years I worked in Manhattan, I would arrive in the city very early each morning. At that hour, I witnessed the hidden side of what makes a city tick, all the support services like washing down sidewalks, hauling garbage to the curb, watering greenery.

One morning as I passed an apartment complex, I stopped to tell the landscaper how much I appreciated the color and variety of blooms he tended so faithfully. His eyes filled with tears as he told me he often struggled with questions about whether his work made any difference to the people passing by.

As we focus our reflection on the suffering of Jesus, we remember that Jesus struggled, as probably all of us at some time do, with doubt. If we wonder whether we are making an impact for good, let us revisit these words from Isaiah.

Sr. Chris Koellhoffer, I.H.M.

GREAT EXPECTATIONS

Then Peter took [the man crippled from birth] by the right hand and raised him up, and immediately his feet and ankles grew strong. Acts 3:7

The man crippled from birth expected little—a coin or two, perhaps, or a cloak or pair of sandals. Imagine his surprise when, instead, Peter healed him in Christ's name.

Sometimes we also expect little when we approach the Father. We focus our prayers and cries for tangible assistance—physical healing, romance, a new job—instead of trusting in him on the specifics. God knows far better than we ever could just how our needs could be addressed best. May we remember that setting aside our own expectations and simply asking for the Lord's grace and guidance will bring us strength and wealth and comfort beyond anything we can imagine.

Lord, I love and trust you. May your will be done.

Melanie Rigney

On a Dark Night, a Cry of Victory

**My strength and courage is the LORD,
and he has been my savior.** Psalm 118:14

Adapting the imagery of Psalm 118, we may picture Jesus standing at the gates of heaven, declaring his conquest of darkness and death. But it is not always easy to enter wholeheartedly into this heavenly celebration. At times, Jesus' victory seems distant from the realities we are dealing with—sickness, anxiety over children, personal conflicts, addictions, bereavement, whatever. We would dearly like to see him overturning the powers of evil—or at least we would like to escape our responsibility to struggle against them—but the problems continue, and we soldier on.

It is helpful to consider the last occasion when Jesus prayed Psalm 118: after the Last Supper, perhaps as he and the disciples were walking to Gethsemane. As he sang the psalm, he knew that he would triumph over death and evil if only by suffering defeat on the cross. The road by which we come to share his victory likewise leads to Gethsemane. When our life is tending in that direction, Jesus walks beside us and offers us this psalm to pray, as an expression of our faith in him.

Kevin Perrotta

October 29

'MIGHTY DEEDS' AND 'FAITH'

And he did not work many mighty deeds there because of their lack of faith. Matthew 13:58

For Jesus, the faith of those around him had a major connection with whether miraculous cures happened. Matthew says here that, indeed, Jesus didn't "work many mighty deeds," not because he couldn't, but because of "their lack of faith."

What are the "mighty deeds" Matthew refers to? What does Matthew mean by "faith"? We can take for granted that mighty deeds refers to miraculous cures, based on Jesus' actions in other gospel settings. But what about faith? And why did he require faith in order to do mighty deeds?

One might think Jesus would want to work miracles by the dozens, all over the place, whenever possible. Would doing this not attract more people to believe in and follow him? Nope. For Jesus, "mighty deeds" depend on faith, not vice versa.

Lord Jesus, help me to entrust myself to you and leave all else in your hands.

Mitch Finley

'YOU ARE HOME'

> While he was with them at table, he took bread, said the blessing, broke it, and gave it to them. With that their eyes were opened and they recognized him... Luke 24:30-31

A consistent feature of the resurrection stories is that the risen Jesus is not immediately recognizable. Something had to happen to reveal that it was Jesus right there with them.

I think this keeps happening. Recently for me it was in a hospital after surgery. Far greater than my apprehension about the surgery was my fear of struggling with post-op nausea and pain in a room with someone who kept the TV blaring on some violent program or scathing talk show. I'd been with family trapped like that.

Wheeled in from the recovery area, I discovered I had my own room with warm yellow walls—the color of my room in the home where I raised my children long ago. The floor was the same terrazzo pattern as the kitchen in that house! In that moment I recognized that Jesus was saying, "I am right here. You are home."

Patricia Livingston

That I May Be Healed

"What do you want me to do for you?" The blind man replied to him, "Master, I want to see." Jesus told him, "Go your way; your faith has saved you." Mark 10:51-52

Imagine the tremendous joy this man felt when Jesus healed his darkness and enabled him to see. But before the blind man could receive this gift, he had to recognize and acknowledge his need for healing. That's an important lesson this story holds for us.

We are all blessed with our share of God-given gifts, but mixed in with those can be a need for healing we don't clearly see. Be thankful for the gifts, but pray for the honesty to recognize and acknowledge what needs to be healed. We can trust that this prayer will be answered. Then the healing can take root, and our transformation can begin.

Lord, that I may see and be healed!

Fr. Kenneth E. Grabner, C.S.C.

At Peace With God

> Their passing away was thought an affliction and their going
> forth from us, utter destruction. But they are in peace.
>
> Wisdom 3:2-3

In Mexico, All Souls' Day is the culmination of a three-day observance commemorating the faithful departed. It is called Día de
los Muertos, Day of the Dead. It is a national holiday with special
foods, parades and even joyous celebration. It is also a very Catholic celebration. After a morning Mass, families go to the parish
cemetery to clean and decorate the graves of relatives with flowers
and remembrances.

For many of us (including me), this kind of celebratory spirit
strikes us as somewhat inappropriate. When we recall those who
have gone before us, our first emotion is one of sadness, not joy.
While we may believe wholeheartedly in the resurrection of the
dead, we miss them terribly. Indeed, their passing is "thought an
affliction." Perhaps we can learn from our Mexican brothers and
sisters that we can hope and trust that our loved ones are now "in
peace" with God.

Paul Pennick

Suffering
Transforms Us

For to this you have been called, because Christ also suffered for you, leaving you an example that you should follow in his footsteps. 1 Peter 2:21

Suffering is to be found in every phase of life, and it will be evident in the life of anyone who faithfully follows Jesus. It is not a punishment or penalty, but an ordinary part of earthly existence. Patient suffering can be a shock absorber that helps us over the potholes and rough places of life without becoming all shaken up. When we accept our hardships without constantly complaining, we weaken their negative impact.

Whether physical, mental or emotional hurts, the better we endure the cross, the more Christ-like we become. Accepting suffering means not running *toward* it, but *through* it. Jesus speaks of a mother forgetting her labor pains once the child is born. Some saintly people have welcomed suffering as a way of imitating Jesus and proving their love for him. Our Savior has said we will save our souls through patient endurance.

Thanks, Jesus, for your suffering to save us.

Fr. James McKarns

Challenging the Status Quo

> So when Peter went up to Jerusalem the circumcised believers confronted him, saying, "You entered the house of uncircumcised people and ate with them." Acts 11:2

Growing up in the 1960s, I remember sitting with an African-American friend watching with horror as the race riots unfolded on television. The experience of watching the pain in my friend's eyes made me aware of the evil of injustice at an early age.

I didn't realize it at the time, but I know now that the abhorrence I felt was the Holy Spirit working within my heart and mind. Through the ages, the Spirit has inspired people to challenge the status quo, risk being misunderstood and even admonished.

Our first inclination is to lash out at our critics, but Peter took a different path. Instead of becoming defensive or self-righteous, Peter explained in detail the extraordinary events and circumstances that led up to his decision to baptize the Gentiles without instructing them in the Jewish law. Peter stood his ground, but he did so in a way that allowed the conversation to continue in a constructive way.

Terri Mifek

November 4

'Getting to Know You'

Jesus said to him, "Have I been with you for so long a time and you still do not know me, Philip?" John 14:9

I have often used the lyrics of the song "Getting to Know You" from the famous musical *The King and I* in connection with God. Through various life experiences, I am constantly getting to know God better. I feel free to express my own thoughts and words without fear or hesitation. As my confidence in God's goodness grows, my soul feels free and easy in the presence of my Savior.

When I think of the Lord as the King of the Universe, it makes the world around me even more bright and beautiful. I want to keep learning more about God, day by day from Scripture, prayer, meditation and through associating with my sisters and brothers. I'm also often telling my King that I'm more and more "getting to like you and getting to hope you like me."

Fr. James McKarns

No Substitute
for God

Not to us, O Lord, not to us
but to your name give glory... Psalm 115:1

At Lystra, Paul and Barnabas cure a man who was lame from birth. One moment he's sitting immobile on the ground; the next minute he's strutting around on his newly restored legs. As a result of the cure, the crowds think that Paul and Barnabas are gods "come down in human form." Paul frantically tries to explain to them that they are not gods but mere mortals. And the cure came not from them but from the "living God, who made heaven and earth."

At times we are like the people of Lystra. We tend to worship "idols," mere mortals who possess talents we revere: the ability to sing, act, play a certain sport, create incredible inventions or just make a lot of money. Even in our Church, we sometimes idolize a certain pope, pastor, popular speaker or spiritual writer. Although it's fine to admire individuals, we must never substitute a "mere mortal" for the one, true living God.

Loving God, I know that only you are the one, true living God.

Sr. Melannie Svoboda, S.N.D.

Seeking and Finding Peace

My peace I give to you. John 14:27

The establishment of global and lasting peace is not possible through human efforts alone. Our hopes for peace cannot rely solely on our treaties, our disarmaments, our defensive weaponry. These only delay the inevitable crisis that will nullify what was once ratified. Peace cannot exist as a deterrent to violence or as a temporary calm in the midst of a hurricane. True peace is God's gift to us, an openness to that which we cannot manufacture by our own efforts. It is given as a gift.

The living and true gift of peace lives in the hearts of those who work for its realization here on earth while knowing that its full and lasting presence is yet to come. It is hidden in the creative wisdom and generosity of God. We have in our hearts the very life of God. And that life is the true source of all human efforts toward seeking and finding peace.

Fr. James Stephen Behrens, O.C.S.O.

GRATITUDE

The LORD is good:
his kindness endures forever,
and his faithfulness, to all generations. Psalm 100:5

Some mornings gratitude is easy, isn't it? It is for me at least. Not too much to do, not too many burdens, sun's out, everyone's feeling good. I'm so grateful!

But what about those other mornings, mornings that are the beginnings of long, hard days, when the night before has been marked by stress that hasn't abated? Those mornings of soreness, aches and weakness? The mornings in which the sun might be shining, but it still seems cloudy? Those mornings, grateful prayers and psalms proclaiming the Lord's goodness might not rise so easily to my lips. I might not think even one grateful thought.

Which is exactly why the Church orders life around these psalms and why I try to as well. And it's funny how that works. I may not think I'm grateful, but the minute I say the words, I am.

Lord, thank you. I am so grateful for you and your love.

Amy Welborn

Making Time for Prayer

We went outside the city gate along the river where we thought there would be a place of prayer. Acts 16:13

Paul traveled constantly to preach. He was faithful to prayer even though he was away from home. We may not be traveling far from our home like Paul, but we are usually on our way to some place every day, even if it's just to the mailbox or the backyard. Whether we are going to a doctor's appointment, out to the garden or to the office, bringing children to school or engaged in some other form of movement, each of us has an opportunity to pause and unite with God.

We can always find a place to pray. For Paul it happened to be along a river. I often pray in the airport or in the car. (I call my car "a little hermitage on wheels.") There's no excuse for just floating through the days without a "hello" to God because I am en route somewhere. All I need do is turn my heart toward the Beloved One and make the inner connection.

Sr. Joyce Rupp, O.S.M.

A ROCK, NOT A STUMBLING BLOCK

He said to his disciples, "Things that cause sin will inevitably occur, but woe to the person through whom they occur."

Luke 17:1

It's interesting that this verse does not say, "woe to the person to whom they occur." No, it's *through* whom they occur. Sin naturally brings us to a state of woe because it's all part of the spiritual process of choices and consequences, sowing and reaping. We make poor choices, and we suffer. We repent, and we are redeemed. Praise God.

But here Jesus specifically warns his disciples, and us, that we will surely face sin, but if we cause someone else to sin—watch out! It's one thing to go down a dark path on our own, but if we lure someone else into darkness, we are in even bigger trouble.

To be sure that we are leading others into the light and not away from it, it is worthwhile to pause here and consider our actions and intentions. As believers our responsibility is great. We must use our influence for good, for God's glory. Be a rock for others, not a stumbling block.

Kristin Armstrong

NOVEMBER 10

Mercy Abounds!

Sirs, what must I do to be saved? Acts 16:30

Paul and Silas are unjustly imprisoned, and the jailer is warned to guard them securely. Despite the fact that the prisoners are staked in an inside cell where escape seems impossible, an earthquake throws open the doors of the prison. The jailer assumes the prisoners have escaped and is about to kill himself, presumably to avoid torture, when Paul shouts that all the prisoners have remained. The jailer's immediate response is conversion.

Paul had mercy on the jailer, and mercy is a powerful weapon for good. When mercy is recognized and accepted, the recipient may be moved to a radically different life. Mercy makes clear that our life is not a sum of what we are missing, but of what we have been given. The recognition of mercy inspires gratitude and a desire to pay it forward.

Sadly, we often don't recognize the mercy offered to us—from God, from those who love us and even from those we casually encounter each day. Mercy abounds.

Paige Byrne Shortal

Motivated to Give My All

For "In him we live and move and have our being," as even some of your poets have said... Acts 17:28

This rich statement encompasses the core of my relationship with the Holy One. The thought of being enfolded, surrounded and intertwined with the Beloved inspires my faith. All of who I am, each part of what my life involves, has a connection with God. I was so taken with the beauty of this reality that many years ago I created a chant based on Acts 17:28. This verse sustains me in times of need. Sometimes I sing it out loud, and sometimes I hum it quietly. At other times, I simply let it quietly circle my mind and heart. When I remember how closely united I am with God, I am able to surrender my hesitations and worries.

This verse also prompts me to turn from what lures me into self-centeredness. Because it is in God that I "live and move and have my being," I am motivated to give my all to the One in whose love I exist.

Sr. Joyce Rupp, O.S.M.

BORN TO LOVE

> You are the salt of the earth. But if salt loses its taste... It is no longer good for anything but to be thrown out and trampled underfoot. Matthew 5:13

Salt derived from the Dead Sea in Jesus' time may have been less stable than the salt we use today. Adverse conditions may have robbed it of its flavor. Adverse conditions can change us too. When we encounter real evil in the world many times over the course of a lifetime, it can erode our confidence that there's any point in trying to do good. We can end up jaded and burned out, our capacity for love diminished. We can lose our saltiness.

That's when prayer can put us back in touch with ourselves. We are beings created in the image and likeness of God. It is our nature to love, to do good, to give of ourselves as God does. The world might disappoint us, people might let us down, but we were born to love them anyway.

Loving God, you created us like you. Help us be true to ourselves.

Karla Manternach

SEEING GOD'S FACE

The LORD is just, he loves just deeds;
the upright shall see his face. Psalm 11:7

I have always had a strong interest in the contemplative experience of God's presence in my life. Fourteen of us here at Holy Cross Village have been actively sharing this interest with one another for several years now. We meet twice monthly to watch videos and share discussion of spiritual topics. Our common interest brings us together, and that has caused our friendships to grow.

This same dynamic works in our relationship with God. The upright will see God's face because they have a common interest with God. They share the mind and heart of God, and their attraction to him gives birth to an ever-growing friendship.

God's word in Scripture shows us how to live according to his mind and heart. And in our prayer, the Holy Spirit guides us to live according to his Word. God draws us to himself, and as we grow in likeness to him, we begin to see his face.

Fr. Kenneth Grabner, C.S.C.

Standing With Jesus

Blessed are you… Rejoice and be glad, for your reward will be great in heaven. Matthew 5:11-12

Whenever I read the Beatitudes, I imagine an enormous checkerboard. In this square, the meek. In that one, the merciful—as though everybody can be lumped into categories like that, once and for all.

In fact, each time I read this passage, a different line speaks to me. One time I'm mourning a loss, so I take comfort in the idea that the pain will not last forever. Another time I'm navigating a conflict, so I notice Jesus' words to the peacemakers. On yet another reading, I'm feeling slighted by people who disapprove of my beliefs, so I relate to the persecuted.

When we choose the path of discipleship, we might find ourselves in any of these groups at any time. Maybe that's why Jesus offers encouragement and consolation, no matter where we stand.

Lord Jesus, whatever I'm facing today, help me to stand with you.

Karla Manternach

The Welcome Mat

Jesus looked up [into the sycamore tree] and said to him, "Zacchaeus, come down quickly, for today I must stay at your house." And he came down quickly and received him with joy.

Luke 19:5-6

When was the last time someone invited himself or herself to dinner at your house? Even when the person is someone you love and whose company you enjoy, it's hard to say, "Sure, come on over!" without running through a mental checklist: Is there enough food? Is the carpet vacuumed? Are the newspapers put away?

But God isn't picky about how well we cook or the tidiness of our souls. He'll invite himself in pretty much anywhere. All he asks is that we open ourselves to saying yes to his request, and to the changes that that "yes" will bring to our lives.

Lord, you will always have a place in my house.

Melanie Rigney

November 16

Pondering the Mystery

God so loved the world... John 3:16

These words are some of the most frequently quoted words in the New Testament. They are an important reminder. In this world, so filled with blessings and burdens, joys and sorrows, it is easy to forget the love of our Trinitarian God. When I ponder the Trinity, the words love and mystery come to mind. A Loving Mystery! A Mystery of Love! One of my favorite hymns is "Holy God, We Praise Thy Name." In this song, we sing confidently about owning this mystery. It is true: This mystery of love is ours. It belongs to us, not as something we can put in the bank for safekeeping, but as something we can put into our hearts for safe living.

O Incomprehensible Mystery, we proclaim that because you want us to live forever with Eternal Life flowing through our beings, you sent Jesus to save us from ourselves.

O you who created us, redeemed us and daily sanctify us, we vow to care for this Mystery.

Sr. Macrina Wiederkehr, O.S.B.

Offering No Resistance?

> You have heard that it was said, "An eye for an eye, a tooth for tooth." But I say to you, offer no resistance to one who is evil.
>
> Matthew 5:38-39

Recently, three of my students have been robbed on their way to or from school. One landed in the hospital with injuries, his laptop and skateboard stolen. One had a machete pressed against his neck in the elevator of his building, causing him to surrender his tablet and subway card. The third, waiting for the bus, lost his wallet and phone to an attacker.

This passage from Matthew's Gospel floors me. It has always been for me the most unsettling exhortation of Jesus. When I was the age of these college freshmen, I prayed for strength not to lash out against the verbal cruelties of a troubled peer. Now, many years later, my heart broken for these young men, I feel the stirrings of my own resistance to Jesus' words.

Come, Holy Spirit! Teach me.

Claire J. King

'Love Is a Practice'

Take care not to perform righteous deeds in order that people may see them. Matthew 6:1

Are we able to face the truth about our actions and our heart's intention? No matter how authentic we may think we are, to act with a pure intention is not easy. Missing the mark in this area goes well beyond just performing good deeds in order to be applauded by others. It is possible to find ourselves doing good works only to be accepted by God, to feel good about ourselves, to get someone to stop pestering us. You may want to make your own list of reasons why you might find yourself performing good deeds for the wrong reason.

Of course, we would all like to act with pure hearts. We don't want to juggle mixed motives. The bottom line, of course, is love. It may not be love that gets us out of bed in the morning and sets our feet in the right direction, but it *could be*. Love is a practice. We learn it as we live.

Sr. Macrina Wiederkehr, O.S.B.

From the Heart...

Rejoice, O hearts that seek the Lord! Psalm 105:3

The psalmist is simply saying, in one sense, "Rejoice, O people that seek the Lord!" But that word "hearts" is worth pondering. It suggests, "Rejoice, you who seek the Lord from the heart." If we seek the Lord from the heart, in earnest, we will find him. If we speak to him from the depth of our being, with the certainty that there is nothing more important to us than him—we will find him. We will discover that we have already been found by him.

And this line from the psalm suggests a further reflection. If we seek the Lord in our hearts, becoming attentive to him as he dwells at the center of our being by his infinite grace, we will find him. We will enter into the life he created us for—a relationship of love with the Father, the Son and the Spirit.

This is a profound mystery. Yet it is accessible to us. Each human heart is made to seek the Lord—and rejoice.

Kevin Perrotta

November 20

STORING UP TREASURES

But store up treasures in heaven, where neither moth nor decay destroy, nor thieves break in and steal. Matthew 6:20

What if Jesus is asking his followers to value things differently? Not just things, such as our possessions, but our children, our egos, our health, our bodies' looks and abilities, our reputations, our intellects, memories and accomplishments? Matthew's Gospel tells us that true followers of Jesus have a radically different orientation to our earthly, embodied experience. That which we think of as ours is not ours, but gifts for use in the span of a lifetime.

The life to which we are called is far greater and more real than the life we now experience with our senses. When what we treasure is ravaged by age or sickness, by slander, flood or war, we are called to remember that the Christian lives the present into the unimaginably glorious future, that nothing can come between us and the incomparable, unconditional, infinite love of God.

Claire J. King

SEEING BEYOND OUR 'BEAMS'

Why do you notice the splinter in your brother's eye, but do not perceive the wooden beam in your own eye? Matthew 7:3

In looking at other people's lives, I seem to see so much more clearly than when I look at my own. Why is that?

Jesus is remarking on how easy it is to pick out the faults of others while struggling to see our own. Perhaps, after taking Jesus' words to heart, we could turn this unfortunate tendency a bit and use it to grow in holiness rather than judgment. It could be an interesting exercise.

In short, how would I like to see my best friend act? If I'm tempted to do some evil, what would I tell a friend in a similar situation? I'd probably find it easy to see the good that he or she should do. Turning to myself, I might then avoid the tendency to excuse and rationalize my way into constructing yet one more huge beam.

Lord Jesus, remove the beam in my eye and help me see myself clearly, as you do.

Amy Welborn

God Sees Our Glory

I am made glorious in the sight of the Lord... Isaiah 49:5

I've seen lots of glorious, almost unspeakable beauty in my life—people and places that have literally taken my breath away. I remember watching my bride walk up the aisle almost 34 years ago. I still get a little weak-kneed thinking about my first glimpses of my children and grandson. I've stood awestruck watching the sun set over the ocean or illuminate the red rock formations of northern Arizona. Simply glorious.

Isaiah reminds us that we, too, are glorious because the God of all creation makes us so. God sees us, is mindful of us, and we become as majestic in God's eyes as the southern rim of the Grand Canyon or a great work of art. The beginning of prayer, St. Ignatius says, is to consider that God "beholds" us. It's incredible enough to consider that the God who made everything pays any attention to us at all. It's quite something else to realize he thinks we're glorious.

God of creation, thank you for making me glorious.

Steve Givens

As Yourself

The commandments…are summed up in this saying, [namely] "You shall love your neighbor as yourself." Romans 13:9

People want summaries: Moby Dick in 100 words, the history of the Civil War in ten minutes, computer literacy in three easy steps. Here St. Paul gives us a summary of the Ten Commandments in one sentence: "You shall love your neighbor as yourself." It's so simple and clear. Or is it?

It's the "as yourself" I sometimes have difficulty with. We Christians are so ingrained with the "love your neighbor" part of the sentence that we sometimes forget those last two words. "As yourself" indicates that we must indeed love ourselves. If we hate ourselves or even look down on ourselves, then we will find it next to impossible to reach out to others with a gracious and sincere love. Our faith not only tells us this, so does good psychology.

Today, why not do one specific act of love for yourself? Treat yourself to something you really enjoy doing.

Loving God, help me to live all the words of your single commandment of love.

Sr. Melannie Svoboda, S.N.D.

TO KNOW CHRIST AS KING

[He] received dominion, glory and kingship; all peoples, nations, and languages serve him. Daniel 7:13

This verse from Daniel points toward the end of time when the kingdom Jesus proclaimed will be established in all its fullness to the ends of the earth. But it also points toward an important truth along the way: All that is good, true and beautiful in any nation or culture draws its strength and purpose from God.

The Holy Spirit is actively involved in human life long before a person is aware of it. At a time in my life when I was at best skeptical about the existence of God, I know that the goodness, truth and beauty around me then helped propel me toward Jesus in subtle and mysterious ways.

Great benefits are available to individuals and nations that know Christ as King, but those that do not are not lost. The Holy Spirit sustains the life of Christ in them, preparing for the day they, too, will serve him.

Mark Neilsen

Our Rock, Our Foundation

Everyone who listens to these words of mine and acts on them will be like a wise man who built his house on rock.

Matthew 7:24

We have many choices when it comes to a most important question: On what will we build our lives? Education, common sense, healthy living, wise investments, family: All of these are good to have in the overall plans for our lives. They are, perhaps, the walls and ceilings and floors of our lives. But none of these are strong enough to be the foundations on which the rest is built.

Only the Word of God and a relationship with Jesus, the Incarnate Word of God, have the capacity and strength to provide a foundation that will never falter, a solid rock footing that will never crumble. Only in God is our soul safe and at rest, both now and forever. The rest, however valuable it may be for a while, is shifting sand and the destructible work of our hands.

God, be my rock and my foundation. Be the Word of my life.

Steve Givens

Entering into the Mystery

In all wisdom and insight, he has made known to us the mystery of his will in accord with his favor that he set forth in him.
Ephesians 1:8-9

Ah, how difficult to receive this kind, wise gift of mystery. Mystery can be fearsome, awesome, overwhelming. By its nature, it's too big for us to grasp, impossible to control.

It's tempting to receive another person, not as a mystery waiting to be revealed, but as a means to an end, or an object of suspicion or attachment. The moments when we can allow another to be truly other, limitless and unfathomable, are moments of grace when we forget our fears and encounter God's real presence. That's sacrament: God's presence experienced through physical reality.

Mysterion is the Greek word translated in Latin as *sacramentum*. In sacrament, we enter into the mystery, God's goodwill. It's encountered in one another, in liturgy, above all in Christ himself. For Christ is God, he is redemption, he is the one who makes us adopted daughters and sons. This is the gift. Not a comfortable or controllable gift, but in sacrament, it is touchable and lavish.

Mary Marrocco

A Need to Learn

I did not come to call the righteous but sinners. Matthew 9:13

I remember a tryout for a baseball team many years ago. The coach stood in front of the group of kids and said: "All right, those of you who think you can play this game, take a step forward." Several of us moved up a step. There were still many guys in the back kicking dirt and hanging their heads, looking away. "Ok, you boys in the back, grab your gloves and take any position on the field you want." One of the boys in the group that "could play" piped up: "Um, coach, what about us? I thought you wanted kids who could play." No, the coach replied, "I want kids who want to learn how to play."

Jesus wanted to be with those who needed him and knew their limitations. Jesus knew that the righteous might not listen to his words. Those "without sin" didn't need Jesus; they already had it all figured out. The others, the sinners, wanted—and needed—to learn.

Paul Pennick

Bearing Our Burdens

Come to me...I will give you rest. Matthew 11:28

Just before this scene, Jesus is expressing disappointment because people were criticizing him rather than appreciating his teachings. So he turns to his Father in prayer. He came to realize that many ordinary people were listening and believing in him.

He says to those who are following him, "Come to me, all you who labor and are burdened" (verse 28). And what does he promise them? He does not say, "I will remove your burden," but "I will give you rest. I will help you deal with it." In fact he says, "Take my yoke upon you" (verse 29). That sounds like another burden. But what is a yoke? It's a device to link two oxen or horses together to form a team. Jesus is saying, "You won't have to bear your burden alone. I will be carrying it with you." Then he adds, "Your souls will find rest." You may still have your weariness and your problems, but I will give you a deep interior peace. Because we will then know we are walking with Jesus, our gentle, humble king who bore his burden for love of us.

Fr. Martin Pable, O.F.M. Cap.

NURTURING REVERENCE

Lord, I am not worthy to have you enter under my roof; only say the word and my servant will be healed. Matthew 8:8

By his death and resurrection, Jesus has already spoken the word to heal our souls. But I wonder how many of us really believe it. It doesn't take many conversations about faith and God to discover that most of us walk around reciting our flaws and beating ourselves up for our inadequacies. It's like we're forever stuck in that first phrase: "Lord, I am not worthy..."

Receiving the Eucharist, taking the body of Christ into our own bodies, should replace that sense of unworthiness with a deep reverence for ourselves and each other as part of the living, breathing mystical Body of Christ.

Evidence of this reverence is hard to see, especially after the host has been consumed and we all get in our cars to leave the parking lot. But we can change this. We can use this Advent as a time to nurture reverence for ourselves and each other as the Body of Christ, remembering that God sent his Son to be born in a stable.

Aileen O'Donoghue

God Is With Us

> There will be signs in the sun, the moon, and the stars, and on earth nations will be in dismay... Be vigilant at all times and pray... Luke 21:25, 36

Sometimes we Christians tend to think Jesus came to sing us lullabies, that when things are comfortable, he's with us, and when they get turbulent, we've lost him—like the disciples in the stormy boat. Here this idea gets turned upside down. When powers are shaken, the skies rearranged, nations disturbed—then we know "God is with us." That's what Emmanuel means, the name Mary and Joseph carried with them into Bethlehem. Joseph and Mary's world was not at all comfortable when God decided to be born into it.

Advent asks us to look forward (to the end times), back (to the Bethlehem journey) and within (to our hearts) and discover in all three one thing: God is with us. Emmanuel. Prayer is our ally. We may feel pulled by Christmas preparations, shopping, baking, gathering, hosting, visiting. But preparation for Christ's nativity requires prayer and vigil. Deep within, in the silence of human pain and hope, his word is uttered.

Lord, teach me to pray and keep vigil so that your Word is borne into the world.

Mary Marrocco

An Urgent Message

"A voice of one crying out in the desert: 'Prepare the way of the Lord...'" Luke 3:4

These days the Christian message is usually proclaimed in calm, relaxed tones. We are used to hearing the gospel preached, and we easily fall into a kind of pious ease. Occasionally something will move us, but most of the time, we are comfortable.

John the Baptist is not a comfortable figure. He leaps off the pages of the Bible as a powerful figure with an urgent message. He points at the scribes and Pharisees and calls them a "brood of vipers." He literally screams his message, "Repent, the kingdom of heaven is at hand!"

Thankfully, you and I are not called to live in a desert and survive on locusts and honey as John did. But we might hope and pray for a bit of the same fire that ignited his spirit. This Advent season, we might pray that we are a bit less comfortable with the gospel. Today, its message is no less urgent.

Msgr. Stephen J. Rossetti

December 2

In God's Presence

**Look to the Lord in his strength;
seek to serve him constantly.** Psalm 105:4

A recent retreat centered on awareness of God's presence right here with us in every moment. The director sent us out into the building and grounds to pay attention to that Presence. I sat on a bench under a tree looking for some golden light or listening for lovely birdsong. Suddenly I was distracted by a small green lizard staring up at me with a look of outrage, as if to say: "What are you doing on MY bench?" The last place I was expecting to see God was in a reptile! I pushed myself to actually look back. I swear that the lizard's gaze softened, and suddenly its tongue flipped out and snatched a mosquito that was about to bite my sandaled foot.

Dear God, your challenges are so creative! Now that I've seen your creative presence reflected in a lizard, help me look more lovingly on other aspects of life I consider unwelcome or annoying. Help me to soften my gaze to see your saving presence right here with me.

Patricia Livingston

GOD'S COMPASSION TRIUMPHS

**My heart is overwhelmed,
my pity is stirred.** Hosea 11:8

In one of the most dramatic passages in the Bible, God is portrayed as arguing with himself and changing his mind. This is not evident in the passage we read at Mass because there are some key verses omitted.

But God seems to say, "I just can't do it," as if he suddenly remembers who he is. "I will not give vent to my blazing anger...I will not let the flames consume you" (verse 9).

This is a profoundly comforting Scripture. How many people are staying away from Mass and the sacraments because they fear God has given up on them? This is the hopeful message Pope Francis has conveyed to us: God's mercy and compassion are unbounded. None of us has a perfect record; we are all in need of ongoing conversion. But even more: God's love and welcome are always waiting for us.

Lord, help me to be a sign of hope and healing.

Fr. Martin Pable, O.F.M. Cap.

Shrewdness and Simplicity

Behold, I am sending you like sheep in the midst of wolves; so be shrewd as serpents and simple as doves. Matthew 10:16

Can you picture a "snove," a funny snake + dove animal that seems like it came right out of a 3-D animation studio? Jesus, the consummate teacher, chose the memorable combination of two extremes to emphasize his point, saying that we must possess the characteristics of both: shrewdness and simplicity.

Here Jesus refuses to let Christians view the world as "us vs. them," good guys separate from bad, sheep and wolves. Sheep can't live in the world of wolves. But doves can. Snakes can. Doves can fly above the pack, and snakes can burrow below ground and share their space. I'm guessing some of us are more snake and others, more dove. Today, let us pray for the gifts of holy shrewdness and holy simplicity alike, in perfect balance, as our Savior taught us.

Claire J. King

Being Fertile and Fruitful

> …making [the earth] fertile and fruitful, giving seed to the one who sows and bread to the one who eats… Isaiah 55:10

An orange doesn't look much like an orange pip. A loaf of bread bears little resemblance to a bundle of wheat. Experience, knowledge and understanding tell us one is the fruit of the other.

How often have I protested about something that was happening or something I had to do: leaving a job or a place, saying goodbye to someone I loved, taking up a difficult work. Rarely did I see these moments as seeds God would water and tend until they produced good fruit. He's trustworthy—but he's tricky.

This text from Isaiah has accompanied me through painful, uncertain, frightening, uncomfortable times. It's reminded me how radical trust is and how radically trustworthy God is. He sends rain on the earth, Isaiah says; it becomes fruit and bread. He sends his Word; it returns to him as his will accomplished. His Word is Christ. Could his Word also be fruitful in us?

Mary Marrocco

Choosing to Love Jesus

[Jesus instructed,] "Whoever loves father or mother more than me is not worthy of me, and whoever loves son or daughter more than me is not worthy of me." Matthew 10:37

Scripture scholars tell us that for Jesus, love of God and love of neighbor cannot be separated; we must do both, and when we do one, we do the other. But here Jesus seems to contradict himself, instructing his disciples that we must love him more than we love parents or children. What gives? Perhaps Jesus realized that even one's closest human relationships can get in the way of faithful discipleship. This was especially true for Matthew's Jewish Christian audience, whose parents and offspring may have been scandalized when their grown children or parents converted from Judaism to Christianity. This experience may be relatively rare today, but it can still happen that a choice must be made between unbelieving parents or offspring and Christian discipleship.

Mitch Finley

Mary Brings Us to Jesus

Hail, favored one! The Lord is with you. Luke 1:28

Not long ago, I was asked to edit a book on Mary, so I gathered a group of exemplary priests to share their personal reflections. What emerged was a moving portrait of this "favored" woman and a striking insight into these fine priests.

In this book, we relearn some important things. First, the place of Mary, while subordinate to Jesus, of course, is unique and an integral part of our Christian spirituality. It is God's will that we should honor this woman. In doing so, we are honoring her Son and thus God himself.

Second, I was edified by the strong and heartfelt devotion these men had for their spiritual mother. In some places these days, Mary is not often mentioned. But it was clear that devotion to her is passionately alive.

Today's feast is situated appropriately within Advent. Her role is to bring us to Jesus. As we celebrate this feast and praise this wonderful woman, our hearts are opened a little bit wider for the coming of her divine Son.

Msgr. Stephen J. Rossetti

December 8

Recognizing Jesus

> **When she had said this, she turned around and saw Jesus there, but did not know it was Jesus.** John 20:14

Mary was sobbing at this moment, grieving the gaping loss of her beloved friend and teacher. He was there with her, present in her pain, even if she didn't recognize him.

This makes me consider some of my most broken and desolate moments and wonder if later I will understand that Jesus was right there with me in the apex of my ache. I cannot fathom how Mary did not recognize him after they had spent so much time together. But this thought comforts me, helping me to understand that I may not recognize him either, even though I believe he comes to comfort me. Maybe he comes in the form of a well-timed phone call, a hug or visit from a friend right when I need it most. Just when I think I am unseen or forgotten, he brings me himself.

Lord, I pray for eyes to see you and a heart to recognize you.

Kristin Armstrong

Getting in Touch

**I will praise the name of God in song,
and I will glorify him with thanksgiving.** Psalm 69:31

Like most people, I am surrounded by distractions on a daily basis in the form of cell phones, the Internet and television. No wonder it is so easy to lose touch with the things that really enrich our lives and open our hearts. Just getting quiet and noticing what is going on within me is often the first challenge I face when I feel overwhelmed.

When I was going through a difficult time recently, I happened to play some spiritual music—a practice I had gotten out of the habit of doing in recent years. I quickly remembered how this type of music can help me get in touch with the deeper dimensions of life and enrich my ability to see things through the eyes of faith. Devotional practices don't change God; they change us.

Terri Mifek

TRULY SEEING

Thus says the LORD:
See! Jeremiah 30:18

Growing in the life of the Spirit invites us into a deepening awareness of God at work in our lives. This may be called living in the present moment, mindfulness or living contemplatively. At its heart is the admonition to live the words: "Pay attention!"

Jeremiah pointed out to the exiles of his time that God was bringing hope, urging a despairing people to "see"—with an exclamation point. The restoration of Israel and Judah was already unfolding. Cities once in ruins would be rebuilt; songs of weeping and mourning what had been lost would be replaced by songs of praise. The remnant, the *anawim*, would grow and become many.

No less than in the time of Jeremiah, ours is a God of abundance and hope. We need to pay attention, to stake our lives on the promise of God's faithfulness and to see, truly see, the hand of God at work within and all around us.

Sr. Chris Koellhoffer, I.H.M.

The Answer Is Yes

But Jonah made ready to flee to Tarshish away from the LORD.

Jonah 1:3

At Mass recently, a priest put the whole matter of sin rather succinctly and in a way I can't forget. In referring to Original Sin—and then, the original and unoriginal sin into which all of us fall—he said, "In the garden, human beings looked at their own Creator and said," and here he paused, "No."

Simple and to the point. Tragic, even.

Yes, it can be a challenge to discern God's will and what it is we are called to say "yes" to, but I have found that what helps is that it's not quite as hard to discern when I remember what saying "no" is really all about. It tends to narrow things down.

A community in need of hearing of God's mercy?

A child of God, wounded and bleeding at the side of the road?

Yes? Or no?

Creator God, open my eyes and grant me the grace to say "yes" to you.

Amy Welborn

Your Witness to the Faith

...do not worry about...what your defense will be... Luke 12:11

Most of the time, our silent witness to the faith is best. As we daily go about our lives, practicing our faith, our witness is what people see in us. Our faith, our joy and our love hopefully inspire others to believe.

But there comes a moment in all of our lives when we are called to give explicit testimony. Perhaps it will be in a social gathering when the faith is challenged. Or it might be when we are faced with a difficult decision, challenging our Christian values. Sadly, more than a few Christians in today's world have even witnessed to the faith with the sacrifice of their lives.

It can be a little frightening to anticipate such a moment. Will we be up to it? Will we be ready? Today's Scriptures tell us not to worry. The Holy Spirit will strengthen us and inspire us. How will you witness to your faith today?

Msgr. Stephen J. Rossetti

December 13

Being Surprised

O shepherd of Israel, hearken,
    O guide of the flock of Joseph!
From your throne upon the cherubim, shine forth... Psalm 80:2

Every time I travel to a new place, I end up surprised. Surprised because, inveterate and enthusiastic researcher that I am, I think I have the lay of the land and believe I know what to expect in this new place.

But no matter what it is I'm seeing in the "flesh" for the first time—a cabin in the woods, a cottage by the sea or even some well-known site, familiar from photographs—I'm always surprised. Reality is always a revelation.

During Advent, I must dig deeply and be honest with myself. What is it I think I know about God? And when I encounter him in the flesh, little arms outstretched to me in eternal mercy and love, what will be revealed to me? Am I open to being surprised?

God of love, reveal yourself to me.

Amy Welborn

December 14

Moving Forward With God's Grace

I will lead them to brooks of water, on a level road, so that none shall stumble. Jeremiah 31:9

The importance of a level road becomes quite clear after a season of seemingly unending snow and bitter cold. With the spring thaw comes evidence of the time winter has spent with some of us, as roads appear riddled with potholes both small and gaping. Driving and dodging the big ones becomes a meditation on what needs to be patched, repaired, restored.

Jeremiah tells us that the road of return to God already has all the holes filled in, not with tar or asphalt, but with tenderness. He imagines a huge throng, the blind, the lame, the women carrying new life, all those who are fragile or broken or wounded or weeping—in other words, all of us. And what do we find waiting for us on this sacred highway? Only compassion, and welcome, and the hand of a loving God so that none may stumble.

Sr. Chris Koellhoffer, I.H.M.

DANCE AND SING FOR JOY

Then will the eyes of the blind be opened,
   the ears of the deaf be cleared;
Then will the lame leap like a stag,
   then the tongue of the mute will sing. Isaiah 35:5-6

Let's suppose that the blind eyes being opened are your eyes. Let's assume the ears that are unstopped and cleared for hearing are your ears. The feet leaping like a deer are your feet, and the tongue loosened to sing praise is your tongue! This supposition is not far from the truth. Indeed, these words serve as a proclamation of freedom and joy. These are words that have the power to come true in your life. Advent is such an enriching season, a time for claiming hope and joy as members of your household.

O God of Hope, make of me one of your far-seeing, deep-hearing, spirited-dancing, wholehearted-singing prophets. Drive far away all lethargy and shallowness. Gift me with authenticity and passion.

Sr. Macrina Wiederkehr, O.S.B.

Beyond the Rules

> But the leader of the synagogue, indignant that Jesus had cured on the sabbath, said to the crowd in reply, "There are six days when work should be done. Come on those days to be cured, not on the sabbath day." The Lord said to him in reply, "Hypocrites!" Luke 13:14-15

Maybe the leader of the synagogue was trying to call Jesus out on a technicality here. But the sabbath was also serious business. Those who observed Jewish law closely felt that Jesus was making a mockery of it. If he was a great spiritual leader, why would he break the rules?

Jesus understood that laws are the beginning of morality, not the end. It's not enough to follow the rules. We must also prayerfully consider what God is asking from us in every situation. As followers of Jesus, we must bear in mind his command to love and serve one another. He called us to reach out to those in need, especially the hurt, the poor and the vulnerable—just as he did when he healed the woman in this story.

Lord God, help me to actively seek what is right in every situation.

Karla Manternach

To Be Fully Alive

Owe nothing to anyone, except to love one another.

Romans 13:8

We are all in debt, one way or another. Most of us have financial debt of some sort, but we can also find ourselves in emotional, physical and even spiritual debt. Some of this is good and necessary. In order to move forward, we sometimes need to lean a little on others.

But debt can turn ugly if we find ourselves enslaved to it. Debt that controls is power, and overwhelming power can turn into slavery. So when we lend, we should do so with the earnest desire for the other to succeed, and when we borrow, we must do so in ways that do not enslave us. God sets the tone for our lives in this regard. The creator and giver of all asks nothing in return but our acknowledgment and love. What God wants is for us to be fully alive, and our desires for each other should be the same.

God, help guide me toward healthy relationships with those with whom I lend and borrow.

Steve Givens

December 18

What's in a Name?

> Therefore the Lord himself will give you this sign: the virgin shall be with child, and bear a son, and shall name him Immanuel. Isaiah 7:14

Many who are parents can recall awaiting the birth of a child with great anticipation. Among the prebirth activities was surely a conversation around naming: poring through baby books, testing possible names out on family and friends, considering what it would be like for a child to live into the name selected, maybe even speaking potential names aloud to hear how they sound. Naming, after all, is not a task to be taken lightly. A child carries the significance of a name with all it implies through the rest of life.

Isaiah tells us that the naming of the Redeemer was also a weighty consideration, for this name would be a sign for all ages. The choice of the Savior's name conveys to us that this is a God who knows our wounds, who shares our joys, who is forever Emmanuel, God with us.

Sr. Chris Koellhoffer, I.H.M.

All Will Be Well

**The Lord is close to the brokenhearted;
and those who are crushed in spirit he saves.** Psalm 34:19

We experience the love of God in many different ways, at different times when we have different needs. I am always moved by this idea of God always close, ready to comfort me when I'm brokenhearted, when my spirit is crushed. I imagine a friend or parent, not trying to fix things, just putting an arm around me and gently saying the words Julian of Norwich attributes to Jesus: "All shall be well, and all shall be well, and all manner of thing shall be well." Because everything *is* okay. One notion of suffering is feeling separated from God, unsupported and disconnected. But that is an illusion. God is right here, waiting to put an arm around me and tell me that all is well.

Lord, when events lead me to feel disconnected from you, let me remember that all I need do is turn to you and receive the comfort you're waiting to give.

Phil Fox Rose

December 20

Everyone Belongs

Jesus said in reply "...Has none but this foreigner returned to give thanks to God?" Luke 17:18

We are sometimes quick to label others as "foreigners." Perhaps they dress "funny," speak with a heavy accent, have darker or lighter skin or practice "odd" customs. To the Jews, Samaritans were foreigners. As such, they were looked down upon and discriminated against. They were not welcome in Jewish circles. Yet, amazingly, the Samaritan in Luke's Gospel is the only one who returns to Jesus to give thanks for the cure of his leprosy. And Jesus praises him in front of the astonished crowd, saying, "Stand up and go; your faith has saved you" (verse 19).

Is there anyone in my life right now who I am treating as a "foreigner"? Is there anyone I am avoiding, shunning or excluding from the arc of my love and concern?

Welcoming Jesus, help me to remember that everyone belongs to everyone else.

Sr. Melannie Svoboda, S.N.D.

The Love of God Lasts Forever

**Now if out of joy in their beauty they thought them gods,
let them know how far more excellent is the Lord than
these.** Wisdom 13:3

Beauty brings pleasure. Cherry blossoms blowing, a mother cradling her child, scarlet leaves dancing along the pavement: These things lift my heart. When I don't feel pleasure at nature's beauty, it's usually because emotions like guilt, anxiety or distraction are in my way. Making a conscious decision to notice beauty can be an act of gratitude toward our Creator.

The joy we feel when we notice beauty reveals that God intends our happiness. In this life, we're called to sacrifice often, and many of us must sacrifice to an unbearable extent—but we are assured that if we are willing to lose our lives, we will regain them in the joy of heaven. The Bible is a love story, and it ends with Love triumphant.

But the blossoms decay; the leaves rot. Even the mother ages and dies. These deaths of beauty keep us from idolatry and point us toward the eternal God.

Eve Tushnet

December 22

In a Pinch

...she, from her poverty, has offered her whole livelihood.

Luke 21:4

Ten years ago, I put a wadded-up bill in the collection basket each Sunday morning. It was wadded up because I was ashamed of the small denomination, but it was generally more than I could really afford. For while I was a well-paid government worker, I was also in personal bankruptcy. My monthly take-home pay was about half of my rent payment, and I worked hard as a freelance editor to make up the difference...and to have even a little money to put in the basket.

These days, my finances are much improved. But I remember that time—and the story of the widow's mite—as I plan my charitable giving for the coming year. I've learned that God repays us a thousandfold when we're willing to be a bit pinched to help his people.

Lord, thank you for all the love and goodness you provide.

Melanie Rigney

SING PRAISE TO THE LORD

Ice and snow, bless the Lord... Lightnings and clouds, bless the Lord. Daniel 3:70, 73

"Blessing" isn't always the first word that comes to mind amid icy cold, thunderstorms and dark days. Yet this song tells us that, in such events, we can come to know God's goodness.

This astonishing song of praise and blessing was sung by three young men flung into a furnace to be burned alive in punishment for their faith. In that desperate place, God brings a fresh breeze that saves their lives. They come to see that he's in all places and filling all things, even the ones that bring pain.

When we start to recognize God's goodness in all things, in the delightful and the unbearable, our hearts expand. Then what have we to fear? How can we not sing and dance, like the three young men in the furnace and Daniel in the lion's den? Nothing will keep us from the love of God. With them and with one another, let's praise and exalt him above all forever.

Let the earth bless the Lord.

Mary Marrocco

Making Room for Jesus

We saw his glory... John 1:14

BLESSED ARE YOU! Christmas day can be so crowded that it is easy to forget its profound spiritual significance. You have chosen to spend the time to read this little reflection and to recall the sacredness of this day.

There can be many reasons to be glad on the greatest of holidays, but most of all we recall the events at Bethlehem. As we meditate upon the scene, a profound peace and joy well up in our hearts. How blessed are we!

Thank you for being present today to the events at Bethlehem. Thank you for remembering Joseph, Mary and the Child. Thank you for making room in your heart for Jesus.

Msgr. Stephen J. Rossetti

Healing Words

Heaven and earth will pass away, but my words will not pass away. Luke 21:33

Some years ago I made an embarrassing blunder while reading a Scripture passage at a Sunday liturgy. I was especially mortified since it took place in a small chapel at a monastery filled with a dozen nuns, a number of lay leaders as well as a few priests. When I sat down, I mumbled to a friend that I was totally humiliated. He smiled warmly and said, "Your mistake was endearing." Those words and the way in which they were delivered were so healing that I consider them some of the most powerful ever spoken to me.

We have an opportunity to be channels of God's enduring love and mercy by how we communicate with one another. I easily forget that when fear and resentment tempt me to withhold an understanding word, but recalling the generosity of others toward me helps to lower my defenses and open my heart.

Terri Mifek

Called to Justice

**He guides the humble to justice,
he teaches the humble his way.** Psalm 25:9

In our quest for world peace, there is one essential quality that is missing. This will cause our failure if we ignore it. The missing piece is justice, which must be the foundation of all moral structures. Jesus says in the Sermon on the Mount that we are to hunger and thirst for justice. It is often called righteousness—a right relationship with God, others, self and all creation. Justice is balanced, extremely fair and unbiased. It is recognized as the hallmark of equity. In our community, country and world, righteousness obliges us to respect others' rights. Justice is to be motivated by the truth, not by what is expedient, clever or profitable. The fair-minded person does not play favorites. The old proverb says that the court may sometimes be most merciful when the accused is most rich. Justice without peace is like oxygen without breath. Nearly 7.4 billion inhabitants have a birthright on the planet.

O Lord, help us to remember and respect that justice is not just for us.

Fr. James McKarns

The Fruit of God's Grace

He is like a tree
planted near running water,
That yields its fruit in due season,
and whose leaves never fade. Psalm 1:3

I count on God's grace to water the roots of my faith. The grace comes in a variety of ways. Prayer, of course, and joining with my parish community to receive the Eucharist help me to be open to God's grace. Like the tree near running water, I must plant myself where the running water flows. Unlike the tree, I have the choice of leaving the rich bank near the stream of God's grace. I have found that my spiritual life grows in direct proportion to how much effort I put into it. If I want my Christian life to yield more fruit, I need abundant grace to help me build my relationships with others and with God. Will I ever be the tree with evergreen leaves bearing great fruit? I hope so, but it isn't likely unless I have well-watered roots of faith.

Deborah Meister

Famous Last Words

Lord Jesus, receive my spirit. Acts 7:59

These last words of St. Stephen, the first martyr, are a beautiful expression of his unwavering faith. As Catholics, we pray for a beautiful death. Being brutally killed doesn't fit our understanding of that, but Stephen's was a beautiful death because his faith remained strong. We'd like to imagine passing away when we are quite elderly, surrounded by loving family members. We'd offer tear-filled good-byes and, like Stephen, ask God to receive our spirit. Yet many do not get such an opportunity. Our Savior, whose birth we joyously celebrate in this season, was murdered at age 33. People have heart attacks; kindergartners succumb to cancer. And, still today, people are martyred.

Perhaps in advance of our final moments, keeping our newborn Savior in mind, we can attempt to build our own unwavering faith by regularly offering a modified version of the prayer that Stephen uttered.

Lord Jesus, I humbly pray that at the hour of my death, you will receive my spirit.

Terence Hegarty

Not Out of the Question

For gracious merciful is [the Lord], slow to anger, rich in kindness, and relenting in punishment. Perhaps he will again relent... Joel 2:13-14

"Perhaps" God will relent: Is it a lack of faith to suggest that God might actually punish us, or, on the other hand, is it presumptuous to say that God would never punish us, no matter how richly we deserved it? The prophet's urgent call to repentance is rooted not so much in fear of the Lord as in the conviction that we have done enough to merit some kind of punitive response. We have, plainly, sinned.

What now? Believing in the unfathomable depth of God's mercy, perhaps we can open our hearts to face our sins and, yes, even the possibility that we deserve punishment. Perhaps we can ask God's forgiveness and receive it in gratitude.

Lord, I have sinned. Set me free to love and serve both you and my neighbor.

Mark Neilsen

December 30

When Is the End?

What have you to do with us, Son of God? Have you come here to torment us before the appointed time? Matthew 8:29

Some gamble their lives on the chance that the end of days never comes. These demons lived by a similar philosophy, and Jesus revealed their folly by bringing judgment to the moment. The demons immediately "pleaded with him"; they knew their fate, but they weren't prepared for it.

We, too, are familiar with this mind-set. We are told to stay awake and prepare ourselves for the kingdom rather than this life. Yet we sometimes treat death as if it were controllable. Even this world points to the contrary—sudden illnesses, unexpected job losses, violent crimes, accidents.

Jesus predicted his own death, and he spent his time speaking the truth and caring for others. If we follow his lead, the end might not be so frightening; indeed, it may be a source of hope.

May I use this life to prepare for the next, Lord.

Julia DiSalvo

Prayers

MORNING PRAYERS

Almighty and eternal God, you have created all things according to your plan from before the beginning of time. I pray in thanksgiving for this day and ask you to help me receive its graces and respond to its challenges. May all that I do serve you and give you glory. Amen.

Jesus, even in the freshness of morning, it is all too easy to take another day for granted. Help me to savor this moment and to cherish the gift of life, even in difficult times. I know that your promises are the only guarantees life holds for us. So help me to appreciate what I have, especially the people you have put in my life. May I never lose sight of how precious my time with them really is.
Amen.

Lord, this morning I am filled with hope for what the day will bring. Be with me as I go about my activities and keep me mindful of your love and care. Thank you for the opportunities you have given me, and may I always act according to your will. Amen.

Heavenly Father, with each new day you bestow on me countless opportunities to grow in your love. Some mornings my worries awake with me, keeping me from appreciating your great glory. Please guide me through the day ahead without needless worry so that I may keep you foremost in my thoughts. Amen.

Lord, out of your desire to share your goodness, you have given me another breath and created another day. May I pause occasionally today and take a deep breath, reminded of the gift of life. May I thank you for all your gifts. Amen.

Lord Jesus, thank you for the gift of life and for the refreshment of a good night's sleep. Renewed to face the day, I have much to accomplish in these next few hours. Strengthen me as I go about my day, and help me to pause to acknowledge you as the source of all that is good in the world. May I serve you today and each day of my life until you call me home. Amen.

EVENING PRAYERS

Lord, free me from the cares of the day so that I can receive much needed rest. Let me not worry about all that is out of my control, but instead, trust in you. I pray that tomorrow will present new opportunities to change what I can and to accept what I cannot. I place my hope in you and pray that I will never be parted from you. Amen.

Good and gracious God, thank you for this day with all its blessings and challenges. Pardon me for the times I closed my heart to your presence and missed an opportunity to be a channel of your love. For the times your presence brought me light and a gentle spirit, I thank you. May I sleep well tonight, trusting in your unending care for me and those I love. Amen.

O God, into your hands I commend my spirit as I lay down for a good night's rest. Hold my loved ones in your heart and touch them with your peace and joy. Be with those who are sick, especially the dying and those who will care for them tonight. Amen.

Almighty and eternal God, as this day draws to a close, I ask your blessing and I pray for a night of rest. I offer you the cares of my day and place in your hands all those for whom I have promised to pray. I know that in your mercy and providence you give each one of us exactly what we need from moment to moment. As I offer my own personal intentions in prayer, grant me the ability to trust in you no matter what happens. I ask this in Jesus' name. Amen.

As I prepare to sleep this evening, Heavenly Father, others are preparing for work. I thank you for the gift of police officers, firefighters, nurses, doctors and others. Bless them for their efforts to keep us from harm and guide them safely through this night. May they undertake their work with your justice and love in their hearts, allowing me to enjoy a peaceful night's rest. Amen.

Gracious God, my mind is filled tonight with memories of what has happened and concerns about what is to come. Much of what fills my heart right now I can do nothing about, and tomorrow is soon enough to take action where it is needed. Now is the time for rest, and so I place myself in your hands and trust in your mercy. Grant me a good night's sleep, secure in your eternal love for me. Amen.

FOR COURAGE

Lord Jesus, you were an innocent victim of violence, and your courage in the face of death opened the way to eternal life for us. Open our hearts now to the Holy Spirit's gift of courage that we may receive new life without fear. Amen.

FOR HEALING OF RESENTMENTS

Lord, you know both the wounds I carry and the grudges I nurse. Bring healing to my heart so I don't have to endlessly revisit old pains and resentments. Help me to forgive, for my own peace of mind if nothing else. Remind me that when you forgive me, the past is released once and for all. May I let go of all the burdens of the past so I can live in joy today. AMEN.

FOR A FRUITFUL LENT

Holy Spirit, lead me into the forty days of Lent as you led Jesus into the desert to confront Satan. Be with me as I confront my own temptations and my failures to live out the promises of my baptism. Give me insight and courage so that I can face the truth about myself and turn back to God in fidelity to the gospel. I ask this in the name of Jesus, my Lord and Savior. AMEN.

FOR EASTER

Lord Jesus, the great feast of Easter reminds us that you came to bring new life to all of creation and share with us your own eternal life. Open our hearts to embrace all your gifts so we may be transformed in your image to become all that you want us to be. May these days of the Easter Season strengthen our trust in your promise of eternal life and our resolve to seek your will in all things. AMEN.

PRAYER FOR MOTHERS

Loving God, bless the mothers among us. Accompany them in ushering new life into our world. Support them in cherishing what is vulnerable and fragile. Enlighten them in mentoring growing lives in the way of peace. Hold in your tender embrace these givers of nurturing love who embody your presence here and now and all the days of their lives. Amen.

PRAYER FOR FATHERS

Loving God, bless the fathers among us. Guide their steps as they learn the ways of wisdom. Strengthen their courage as they choose and protect what is right and just. Deepen their capacity for loving service as they live into the vocation of parenting that, like your own divine love, endures day in and day out. Amen.

FOR INACTIVE CATHOLICS

Lord Jesus, for a variety of reasons, many people who once worshiped as faithful Catholics no longer attend Mass, receive the sacraments or embrace the faith. May your Holy Spirit continue to reach out to them, and may they always find in the Church a community ready to receive them once more, hear their concerns and grow together in faith. Amen.

FOR ADVENT

Lord Jesus, you said that you came not to condemn the world but that we might have abundant life. Open my heart to receive the abundant life you offer me this Advent season. Allow me to experience the wonder of a child looking forward to Christmas for the first time. Strengthen my desire for your coming that I might be renewed in heart, mind and spirit as I prepare to celebrate your coming at Christmas. AMEN.

FOR CHRISTMAS

Word Made Flesh, you came to share our humanity so that we might share your divinity through baptism. Though it is more than we will ever fully understand, the miracle of your birth gives gladness to our hearts. As our voices rise in praise throughout this Christmas season, we pray that the good news of your birth might spread far and wide. May we, by word and deed, give witness to your continuing presence in a world that is sorely in need of your love. AMEN.